Retire Happy!

Tom

DON'T WORRY,

RETIRE HAPPY!

*Seven Steps to
Retirement Security*

TOM HEGNA

Foreword by Kelvin Boston

Copyright

Table of Contents

Acknowledgements ——————————————————— i

Foreword ——————————————————————— v

Preface ————————————————————————— ix

Introduction: The Importance of Happiness in Retirement ——— xix

Step 1: What is Your Plan? ——————————————— 1

Step2: Maximize Social Security Benefits ————————— 21

Step 3: Explore a Hybrid Retirement ————————— 39

Step 4: Protect Your Savings from Inflation ——————— 51

Step 5: Secure More Guaranteed Lifetime Income ————— 61

Step 6: You Must Have a Plan for Long Term Care ———— 79

Step 7: Use Home Equity Wisely ——————————— 97

Some Extra Tips for Those Who Have Started Late ———— 105

A Special Note to Women ——————————————— 115

Retirement Issues for Non-Traditional Couples ————— 127

Using "Longevity Credits" for Retirement Income ———— 133

What Does Life Insurance Have To Do With Retirement? —— 143

Conclusion ———————————————————————— 165

Sources ————————————————————————— 170

Acknowledgements

There are a number of people I would like to recognize for their contributions to this book. First, Kelvin Boston, since none of this would have happened without his active role in getting a "Don't Worry, Retire Happy!" Public Television Special. Susan Wright, CLU, ChFC, RHU, REBC, ADPA, helped me draft the book and Andrea Weidknecht helped me edit the book. I also want to thank Jim Bricker, MBA, Financial Advisor, who really has helped me with all three books. He has a sharp eye and an incredible attention to detail. He has proofreading and editing skills that have been extremely valuable to me.

This book has been a real journey. The first step was scripting the TV Special. That script formed the basis of this book. We then added key concepts from both "Paychecks and Playchecks: Retirement Solutions for Life" and "Retirement Income Masters: Secrets of the Pros." We also added significant portions to the Social Security chapter, and the Chapters on Women, Late Starters and Non-Traditional Families. I want to recognize Brandon Buckingham of Prudential. He is an incredible speaker on the subject of Social Security and blended some of his information into that chapter and the Social Security Guide we did for the TV Special.

My regular travel and speaking schedules don't leave me with a great deal of additional time, so the assistance of these wonderful people helped to get this book out to you in a much more timely manner than would have been otherwise possible. I also want to thank Robby Roussel, who schedules all of my events. I can't do what I do without him. Also my family, for the sacrifices that they make because of my significant absences. They know that I am on a mission to try to save as many people as possible from a sub-optimal and unhappy retirement.

The process that we used was one that was familiar, as Susan, Andrea, and I had used a somewhat similar course of action with my previous book, "Retirement Income Masters: Secrets of the Pros."

Using information that I provided from my research, Susan Wright was able to weave in additional statistics and data and then provide me with a basic framework for each of the book's chapters. She would send each chapter as it was completed and from there, I would add, delete, and revise, providing my own voice and advice to the information.

I would then send my draft of each chapter on to the editor, Andrea Weidknecht, who then restructured the material into a standardized storyline. I asked Jim Bricker to do a final proofread and then he sent it back to me for any of my finalized edits. After adding Kelvin Boston's Foreword, we had a complete book.

Once we were set with our content, the necessary legal and compliance reviews were conducted in order to ensure that all of the i's were dotted and t's were crossed. You can never be too careful when discussing financial information.

In all, while the process always seemed to involve a number of back-and-forth steps, I believe that the end result is something that will be truly beneficial to you.

I would also be remiss if I didn't acknowledge the great professionals who created the television special – of course Kelvin Boston, but also Alan Foster, Dennis Allen, Bob Comiskey and their professional teams. Thanks to Gary David Gold Photography for all of the great pictures from the set. The sponsor of the TV Special is a Fortune 100 company that likes to remain out of the spotlight, but I sincerely thank them for all of their support.

Finally, to my fellow road warriors around the country who spend months away from their families so that other families can handle their finances more wisely and retire more successfully – people like Joe Jordan, Anthony Morris, Van Mueller, and so many other top speakers around the country.

The steps that are presented in this book will help to guide you toward a rewarding and hopefully very happy and worry-free retirement!

Foreword

Financial dignity is the term that may best summarize my professional career. That is because most of my work has focused on just that - helping people live their lives with financial dignity. This is the same mission of the Moneywise television series that I host and produce for public television, and it was the thought that stirred my emotions the first time I saw Tom Hegna speak at a GAMA meeting in San Diego, California in 2013.

Tom's presentation was quite frankly spell-binding. He held the attention of 3,000 financial services leaders in the palm of his hand. Even though we all knew about annuities, few of us really understood the role that annuities really played in providing people with lifetime retirement security. Tom's speaking skills were amazing, and his information was life changing! His message was hot! In fact, he closed his presentation with real flames coming from the pages of his bestselling book at the time, Paychecks and Playchecks.

I had been a financial advisor, author, and media professional in the financial niche for many years, but this was still the first time I had ever heard someone explain how retirees could secure their retirement income for life. Tom got a standing ovation for his presentation. Afterwards, I tracked him down at his jam-packed convention booth where he was signing books and taking dates for local speaking engagements. Most of the conference attendees understood that Tom Hegna could help them build their financial services business. But, I understood how Tom Hegna's information could help me to help millions of American retirees live their lives with financial dignity.

I asked Tom if he would consider doing a national public television special. He said yes, and we started working on the Don't Worry, Retire Happy public television special. The book you are reading is the positive outcome of our work. I am very proud of the public television special and of this book, Don't Worry, Retire Happy: Seven Steps to Retirement Security. Both the special and the book outline seven basic steps that people need to understand in order to secure their retirement.

Naturally, there is only so much information that you can share in an hour-long television program. So, the book has more information that can help you to understand how to implement the seven steps to your secure retirement. In each chapter, you will find valuable information that Tom Hegna has used to help countless Americans enjoy their retirement over the years. Thanks to our collaboration on the Don't Worry, Retire Happy television special, Tom Hegna has generously allowed me to also include some insights from my years as a financial journalist in this book.

In this book, you will find new retirement planning concepts like hybrid retirement, Social Security maximization, secure guaranteed lifetime income, planning for long-term care, and more. We included these and other retirement strategies because they will help you to enjoy a worry-free and happy retirement.

According to AARP, in 2015, 45 percent of the United States population will be over the age of 55. Both Tom and I are proud to be members of this Baby Boomer generation. We are also passionate about helping this generation and others to enjoy a happy retirement. We have read the studies which cite that pre-retirees' biggest fears are running out of money during retirement or outliving their retirement savings. We also understand that retirement security must be an achievable goal experienced by all Americans, regardless of their income, investment savvy, or net worth.

Few schools in America teach children the basics of financial planning. Even fewer colleges teach adult Americans the basics of retirement planning. Don't Worry, Retire Happy was written with this in mind. It will provide you with the basic information you need to understand and to reach your retirement goals.

Don't Worry, Retire Happy - that is the focus of this book. No book can absolutely guarantee that you will be happy when you retire. The science of happiness tells us that only you can control your emotions. Still, understanding how to secure your retirement will reduce your retirement fears and help you to enjoy more peace of mind after you retire.

To me, having retirement peace of mind is living your life with financial dignity. This is the seed that helped produce Don't Worry, Retire Happy: Seven Steps to Retirement Security. This is the opportunity that Don't Worry, Retire Happy offers you. This is the worry-free and happy retirement that I hope you will enjoy.

The book you have opened contains information that will help you live your retirement with joy, happiness, and financial peace of mind. I truly hope that you enjoy reading it and enjoy taking your steps to a worry-free and happy retirement.

Kelvin E. Boston
Moneywise Television Series
Host and Executive Producer

Preface

You can stop worrying about retirement. You are about to find your own Happily Ever After. With *Don't Worry, Retire Happy! Seven Steps to Retirement Security,* I will give you all of the tools you need to live an OPTIMAL retirement.

Let's clarify. Optimal does not mean "best." No one knows what the *best* will be: If gold soared to $25,000 per ounce, we would wish we had invested in gold; if the Dow Jones hit 100,000 in the next five years, we should have all put our money into the Dow 30 stocks. Optimal simply means the best more often than anything else and that it will never be the worst. Math and science always look for the optimal solution, and we can do just that when it comes to securing a successful retirement. I will lay out the math and science of a successful retirement. I'm not trying to get you to buy a product and I don't represent any single company. I am simply a speaker and an author who has spent more than 25 years in the financial services industry. I have seen success and I have seen failure.

With my help, you can confidently plan to spend your retirement years happy and worry free. A happy retirement is within your grasp. My Don't Worry, Retire Happy Plan and Seven Steps to Retirement Security will put the tools in your hands.

There was a time in this country when you could retire gracefully knowing that the company you worked for had provided for you and your family. But the time of the shiny gold watch and that guaranteed paycheck in the form of a pension is no more. In the early 1980s, over 60 percent of American workers had a pension plan. In 2011, only 18 percent were covered by a guaranteed pension plan. This change from employer-sponsored retirement programs to employee-saving retirement plans is important. The 401(k) and other employee retirement savings plans were initially intended to *supplement* corporate pension plans – not replace them.

Now you know what happened to the "happy retirement": It has been replaced with the worry-filled, do-it-yourself retirement. But, I am here to tell you that retiring happily ever after still does exist, and you can do it!

Retirement has been studied in depth. There is near unanimity by economists as to how retirement income should be structured to give you the very best shot at Happily Ever After. And I am going to share the "secrets" that these experts have discovered.

One of the most interesting observations I've made during my study of retirement is that most of the public discourse about retirement is focused primarily on asset accumulation, or building up retirement savings. Everyone is focused on their "pile of money": *How big can I get the pile?* But there has been very little discussion about retirement *income*.

Retirees don't live on assets, they live on income! Your assets can be lost, they can be stolen, swindled, sued, divorced, or decimated in a market crash. The ultimate success of your retirement is not about assets. It is about income and risk management. This is a huge paradigm shift. It goes against EVERYTHING you have been doing up to this point.

Let's pretend that you and your partner are now retired. You know what you need? You need a paycheck. You can have that paycheck guaranteed or not guaranteed. Which would you prefer?

Now, if you said guaranteed, how *long* do you want it guaranteed for —the rest of *your* life? Or for the rest of *both* your lives?

If you answered guaranteed for the rest of both your lives, you need guaranteed lifetime income.

Let me ask you another question: During your working life, what day of the week do you spend the most money? What day do you go golfing, go to the hardware store, get your nails or your hair done? For most people, that day is Saturday. When you retire, *every day is Saturday*!

You're not just going to need paychecks, you are also going to need some PLAYCHECKS so that you can actually enjoy your retirement! And I can tell you how to get them.

With my Seven Steps to Retirement Security, you will:

- Develop a retirement plan
- Enjoy more Social Security benefits
- Consider a hybrid retirement
- Protect your savings from inflation
- Secure more guaranteed retirement income
- Plan for long-term medical costs
- Use your home equity wisely

Before elaborating on my seven steps, let's review a few of the concerns and risks people face in retirement.

Did you know that there are 78 million baby boomers approaching retirement age? This represents 26 percent of the United States population. You are not alone!

Many baby boomers and many of the rest of you will enter retirement with nowhere near enough money. For whatever reason, your life took an unexpected turn and you find yourself in your fifties or sixties with very little to retire on. However, that does not mean it is too late to enjoy retirement. I will show you some of the 21st-century solutions people are using to eliminate the fear of not having enough money for their retirement. It will not be easy, but the actual case of a 57-year-old woman with more guaranteed lifetime income than she ever had while working may convince you that it is within your reach.

Another concern is that people are living longer than ever before. The life expectancy of a 65-year-old male is age 85; for a 65-year-old female, it is 88. But here is an interesting fact: Married people live longer than single people. I have no idea why a couple's life expectancy becomes 92, but it is a *fact*. There is even a 25 percent chance that one spouse will live to be 97, and some of you reading this book may very well live to 100.

Although everyone wants to live a long life, longevity is not just a risk; it is a *risk multiplier* of other risks in retirement. Market risk, withdrawal rate risk, sequence of returns risk, inflation, deflation, increasing taxes, long-term care – longevity risk is hands down the number one risk in retirement. The longer you live, the more likely the market will crash; the longer you live, the more likely you will withdraw too much money; the longer you live, the more likely inflation will decimate your purchasing power; the longer you live, the more likely you will need long-term care. To retire successfully, you MUST take longevity risk off the table. And I will show you exactly how.

After 2008 and 2009, I think everyone understands market risk. The market was sliced in half. For many people, it happened right before they were to retire. And, to make things worse, many lost money on the way down, then they got out at the bottom and never rode the market back to the new highs of today. What people don't understand is that *when* you lose money may be more important than *how much*.

Let's take Jim. Jim invested 50 percent in stocks and 50 percent in bonds over a 22-year period. Although the market went up and down, the portfolio averaged 10.1 percent. His initial $100,000 investment grew to be worth $846,000. Even if we ran the numbers backward from 1995 to 1973, he still averaged 10.1 percent per year and still wound up happy.

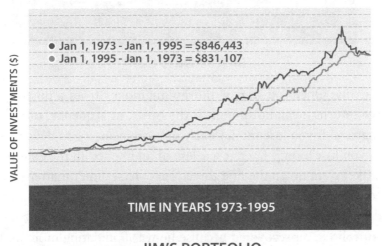

JIM'S PORTFOLIO

This is the way many people (especially stock brokers) think the markets work: Markets go up and down, but over time they always go up. While that is true when you are a saver and an investor, it is NOT true the day you retire and start taking money out of a portfolio.

Now let's take Bill, who invested identically to Jim—50 percent stocks, 50 percent bonds, 10.1 percent average return over 22 years. However, Bill retired that first year. His broker told him he could withdraw 5 percent per year: If he averaged 10.1 percent per year, he could certainly withdraw just 5 percent, right? Wrong. He ran out of money!

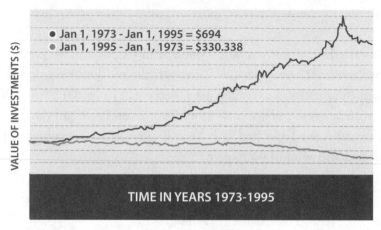

- Jan 1, 1973 - Jan 1, 1995 = $694
- Jan 1, 1995 - Jan 1, 1973 = $330.338

VALUE OF INVESTMENTS ($)

TIME IN YEARS 1973-1995

BILL'S PORTFOLIO

Here is why: Once you start withdrawing money from a portfolio, average returns mean nothing. It is the order, or sequence, of returns that matters. If you lose money *early* in retirement, it can devastate you. If you lose money later, it has less of an impact. In the examples, the market went down the first three years. That didn't matter to Jim since over the 22-year period he still *averaged* 10.1 percent. But Bill withdrew money each year and that money could never grow back. His portfolio never recovered because he was liquidating more and more shares to provide the money he needed in retirement.

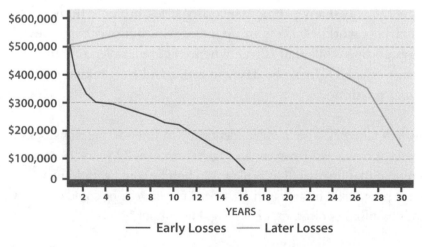

Take a look at this chart. Both of these portfolios have identical average returns. What is the only difference? The dark line lost money early in retirement, which devastated their retirement. The lighter line shows how they lost money later in retirement, which had much less of an impact.

For this reason, the riskiest time to invest is not when you are 87 as many people believe. It is when you are 57 or 67. Losing money right before or right after retirement can devastate your entire retirement. This is why it is so important to have some guarantees in your portfolio.

Another devastating risk is inflation – the silent thief. Over time, it can wipe out purchasing power. Then there is deflation, which is not even on the radar of many Americans. Think about what happened to the housing market over the last five or six years. In many parts of the country, there has been significant deflation. Housing prices crashed; some of those markets are still down. Yea, but Tom, it can't happen here... Don't be so sure.

As an economics major, I get why everyone is so worried about inflation and hyperinflation. The United States has printed TRILLIONS of dollars. Normally, every time you print a dollar, the value of all of the other dollars goes down. We are $18 trillion in debt, climbing at $2 to 3 billion every single day and printing nearly $2 billion every day with a goal to taper to zero by the end of 2014. If you do the math, that doesn't work out well over the long term. So why has the dollar not plummeted? Because we're not the only ones in debt, and we are not the only ones printing money.

Europe's in debt and printing money. Greece is insolvent. Japan has even higher debt-to-GDP ratio than Greece – so some might say that Japan is also insolvent and printing money faster than we are. China's in debt and China is printing. So how does our printing factor out with all of the other printing? Someone smarter than me will have to figure that out, but I will tell you this. We have *never* seen a world where the governments were in debt over $52 trillion dollars.

ONE TRILLION DOLLARS - BY THE NUMBERS

Most people don't really know what a trillion is. After all, it rhymes with million and billion. Here is a very simple way to understand how much a trillion is: If one dollar equals one second, a million dollars would be about 11.5 days, and a billion dollars would be 32 years. A trillion dollars wound be 32,000 years. Isn't that incredible - 32,000 years...

OK, so there is a lot of debt – so what? Well, when you are in debt, eventually you have to get out of debt. I'll bet many of you have been in this situation. You have had credit card debt or student loans. But when you are paying off your debt, what AREN'T you doing with your money? You are not spending it, nor are you saving it. See, paying off debt is very hard on an economy.

So, how does a government get out of debt? There are three ways, and we normally only hear about two of them – raise taxes and cut spending. (The third is growth.) What happens to an economy when you raise taxes and cut spending? It is highly deflationary, not inflationary.

Getting out of debt this way is called deleveraging. Be on the lookout for tax hikes and spending cuts in the world's future. This will significantly limit growth – and may even prevent growth – for decades.
The next problem is demographics. What happens economically when

a country gets old? Their spending goes off a cliff. Just think – after age 50, the kids typically move out (at least for a couple of months), your spending starts going down, and you will typically spend less each year for the rest of your life. This reduction in spending is deflationary, not inflationary. In Japan, they sell more adult diapers than baby diapers. And those 78 million baby boomers in the United States—they are all over age 50 now. They will be spending less and less every year for the rest of their lives, as will an aging Europe and Japan!

One of the brilliant demographers of our time is a gentleman by the name of Harry Dent. Granted, he is controversial and has predicted many things that have not come true. But as a demographer, I find his work second to none. Want to get some chills sent up your spine? Read Harry's book "The Demographic Cliff" on the coming "economic winter." This massive debt, the inevitable deleveraging that must occur, and the aging of the entire world means that DEFLATION, not inflation, may become a common part of your vocabulary. My whole life I believed Milton Friedman when he said "inflation is always and everywhere a monetary event." Meaning, inflation is caused by the printing of money. I believed that for 50 years. I don't believe it anymore. Harry Dent says that inflation is a demographic event! Young countries experience inflation. Old countries experience deflation. Wow—another Paradigm Shift!

This explains how we have printed trillions of dollars yet remain in a low interest rate / low inflation rate environment. It is because America (and much of the developed world) is getting older!

Look, I can't predict the future better than any of you. My best advice is to watch the bond market because it predicts the future every single day. As I am writing this, the 30-year US government bond is paying 3.25 percent. What is the bond market predicting are the odds of any inflation or hyperinflation in this country for the next 30 years? NADA.

Ben Bernanke, the guy running the printing presses in Washington, DC for the past decade, recently spoke at some dinners for the rich and famous. Did you catch what he said? He said that interest rates are unlikely to go over 4 percent for the REST OF OUR LIVES! Why? Because of the deflationary pressures of debt, deleveraging, and demographics. At least consider the risk of deflation. I will show you ways to take it off the table as well.

Another monster risk in retirement is long-term care because it can literally wipe out your entire retirement. I have, again, dedicated an entire chapter to this risk. But here is a preview: NO retirement plan is complete without a plan for long-term care.

A couple of other risks are taxation and regulatory risk. I will do my best to give you some advice, but even Tommy cannot control these risks. The government does what the government does. The best we can do is to elect leaders and representatives who have the country's best interests in mind. Sounds easy, but as we have seen over the past decade, it can be very difficult.

Longevity risk, market risk, debt, demographics, long-term care, taxes, regulatory risk – there are many risks concerning us as we face retirement. When you consider the millions of people approaching retirement who were not able to save as much as they had hoped, it is easy to see why so many Americans are worried about retirement.

Wouldn't it be great if schools taught you how to secure your retirement? But don't you worry; think of this book as your retirement guide. In this book, I will address these risks and you will learn that retiring well does not have to be a fairy tale. Don't Worry, Retire Happy!

Introduction:
The Importance of Happiness
in Retirement

What does "Happily Ever After" even mean? If you've been regularly setting money aside in a 401(k) plan, an IRA account, or some other type of long-term savings plan for the future, why are you doing it? What are you actually saving the money *for*?

If you don't know, you need to. William Bernstein, a neurologist and cofounder of the investment management firm Efficient Frontier Advisors, sums it up best: "Golf is not a plan."

Bernstein also writes, "The biggest mistake retirees make is not having a clear idea of exactly what useful and productive things they're going to do with their time." He provides his own formula for retirement happiness, which looks something like this:

RETIREMENT HAPPINESS =
[HOW MUCH YOU DISLIKE YOUR JOB] X
[HOW BADLY YOU WANT TO DO SOMETHING ELSE]

If you have no clear idea of how badly you want to do something else – or what that "something else" even is – then that goes into the equation as a big zero.

Another crucial factor is the role that retirement savings plays in the equation. If you struggle to pay your bills every month in retirement, the likelihood of you being happy is low. Therefore, laying the groundwork to be able to leave your current job with enough savings to convert into income is essential to your happiness... or is it?

WHAT DETERMINES WHETHER OR NOT
YOU ARE TRULY HAPPY?

While William Bernstein and Libby Kane think that those who have a clear plan of what they will do in retirement are the happiest, there are other experts who would differ. Some say that you need to be happy long *before* you reach retirement in order to be happy *in* retirement.

In other words, there is a great misconception about happiness – some people think that they must first achieve a certain goal before they can be happy, when they actually need to be happy first before they can work toward their goal.

THE REAL KEY TO HAPPINESS IN RETIREMENT

Regardless of which side of the fence you are on, once you reach your retirement years, those people who planned for their retirement are happier than those who did not.

A Northwestern Mutual life insurance survey studied financial discipline and happiness in retirement. They found that people who rated themselves as being "highly disciplined" planners were much more likely than those who were non-planners to say that they were happy in retirement – by a score of 91 percent to 63 percent. This study also found that those who were the planners before they reached retirement were much more likely than the non-planners to feel "very secure" financially.

ATTAINING ONGOING INCOME CAN LEAD
TO LIFELONG HAPPINESS

Believe it or not, there is now an emerging field in the area of economics known as "happiness research." When brainstorming how retirees can improve their odds of a happier retirement, researchers found that one of the results was to "buy yourself income." What exactly does this mean? According to the *Wall Street Journal* and Professor Keith Bender of the University of Wisconsin-Milwaukee, it means that retirees who receive regular income are much happier than those who don't.

In some of my own research, I've found that people who own annuities are happier than those who don't. In fact, those who own annuities are not only happier, they are also more likely to live longer!

The producers of the well-known *Freakonomics* books and radio series of the same name also did a podcast discussing how reliable income from an annuity helped retirees remain happy. They referred to those who lived long lives and collected income checks month after month, year after year, as people who had won the "longevity lotto."

Jane Austen even wrote about the "longevity lotto" in her own way in the classic *Sense and Sensibility:* "If you observe, people always live forever when there is an annuity to be paid to them... The annuity is a very serious business; it comes over and over every year, and there is no getting rid of it."

Then in 2012, *TIME* had the following article: "Lifetime Income Stream Key to Retirement Happiness." It went on to say, "A new study in a land of grumps reveals that retirees with a guaranteed lifetime income stream can find true happiness."

Towers Watson wrote an entire white paper on retirement happiness titled "Annuities and Retirement Happiness." They studied retirees of all ages and incomes and found that the cushioning effect of guaranteed lifetime income allowed retirees to feel more secure and happier in retirement. Some of their key findings were as follows:

- "Retirement satisfaction has steadily declined over the last decade."
- "Satisfaction is highest among those with high levels of wealth and income who are very healthy and annuitize their income."
- "Among retirees with similar wealth and health characteristics, those with annuitized incomes are the happiest."
- "Annuities provide the biggest satisfaction boost to retirees with less wealth and those in poor health."

When I speak at public seminars across the country, I typically ask, "When you retire, do you want to be *happy* or *unhappy*?" At this point, the audience mumbles, "Happy." I counter, "Well, you sure don't sound like it. I'm serious; do you want to be happy or unhappy?" They then respond loudly and enthusiastically, "HAPPY!" Now that they're ready, I show them the *Wall Street Journal* article "The Secret to a Happier Retirement: Friends, Neighbors, and a Fixed Annuity." It lists seven key points to follow to ensure happiness in retirement: "Value your time, think ahead, expect less, pick your neighbors, buy yourself income, work at retirement, and invest in friendship." Notice that one—"buy yourself income"—is about guaranteed income.

Let me tell you a quick story about my own family. I grew up in a small town in Minnesota of 2,500 people. Both of my parents were teachers. Now, if you know anything about teachers and small towns, you know they didn't make much money.

We had all the necessities, but no real luxuries. I had jobs – a paper route, shoveling snow and mowing lawns, and selling popcorn at the county fair. If I wanted a new baseball glove, I bought it. If I wanted a new bike, I bought it. If I wanted to go to a Twins game or a Vikings game or to see the Harlem Globetrotters, I had to sell more subscriptions to the *Minneapolis Star and Tribune* to earn a trip.

(I sold numerous subscriptions and earned many great trips.) That is how I grew up. My parents never made a lot of money, but they had PENSIONS.

My wife's parents, on the other hand, were business owners. They made more money than my parents, but they didn't have pensions. Now that my parents are in their eighties, they have never, not once, expressed concern about running out of money. They don't even think about it. But almost every conversation with my wife's parents deals with their concerns. They have basically run out of money. Why? They had planned on living to life expectancy, which at the time was age 76.

He is now 94, she is 92.

What is the difference between those two sides of my own family? One had guaranteed paychecks for life and the other didn't.

I cannot stress enough the importance of guaranteed lifetime income to your happiness in retirement. Knowing that you will have an income – regardless of what happens in the market – is going to make you less stressed. In turn, that will help to keep you happier and healthier overall.

WHAT ELSE WILL YOU DO IN RETIREMENT?

Once you have a regular stream of income nailed down, you will be able to enjoy everything else that retirement has to offer. But this time in your life won't come without its other challenges. That's why it is important to have a plan that goes beyond just the immediate financial aspects of retirement.

You will need to factor in other items to keep up your happiness in retirement:

KEEPING ON TRACK WITH A PURPOSE

– Once you retire, you may feel that you've lost your purpose. You may have felt a strong sense of association to your employer or career and now, suddenly, being away from it may make you feel at a loss. Therefore, be sure that you've made plans to fill your time, such as travel, volunteering, or even a new career.

REMAIN ACTIVE SOCIALLY

– Remaining active should include regularly keeping in contact with friends and relatives as well as developing new friendships. Many experts agree that a big measurement of whether people are happy in retirement is based on the strength of their social network.

STAY HEALTHY

– Today, life expectancy is longer than ever before, which means that your retirement could last 20 years or more. While this is great news, you will need to make a conscious effort to stay physically and mentally fit. Eat right, exercise, and keep sharp by reading or participating in other cognitive challenges. All of these things can do a body good—and when you feel better, it is much easier to remain positive.

HOW TO WORRY LESS AND RETIRE HAPPIER

Given the fact that planning is such an important part of feeling happy in retirement, it is essential to develop a plan for yourself.
If you don't currently have one, this book will get you on the right track and show you the steps that you need to follow.
If you do have a retirement plan, the information in this book can show you where you may have left any potential gaps – and how to

fill them so that you don't discover them after it's too late. Many of the respondents in the Northwestern Mutual survey who didn't have a plan stated that the reason they didn't have a plan was because they didn't have enough time to develop one. Yet, the average American watches in excess of four hours of television each and every day. Simply reallocating some time to plan for the most important, and likely the longest, "vacation" of your life would be time well spent – time that could help you to worry less and retire much happier.

KEY CHAPTER POINTS

- What are you saving your money for?
- Having a clear idea about how you will be spending your retirement years is crucial to how happy you will be.
- "Golf" is not a plan.
- The biggest mistake that retirees make is not having a clear idea of exactly what useful and productive things they're going to do with their time.
- You need to be happy before retirement in order to be happy in retirement.
- Those who planned for their retirement are happier than those who did not.
- People who own annuities are happier than those who do not – and they are also more likely to live longer, too.
- It is important to have a plan that goes beyond just the immediate financial aspects of retirement.
- Simply reallocating some time to plan for the most important, and likely the longest, "vacation" of your life would be time well spent – time that could help you to worry less and retire much happier.

Step 1: What Is Your Plan?

A retirement plan is the "blueprint" to get you from where you are now financially to where you want to be in the future. Step 1 of the Seven Steps to Retirement Security starts the outline by discussing the importance of having a retirement plan in place.

Too many people today think that they can just "wing it" and be ok. That simply doesn't work. Why? Because there's too much uncertainty when it comes to future income and expense needs. Nobody knows how much they're going to need in retirement nor do they know how long they will need it.

There's also uncertainty surrounding pension benefits and Social Security. Defined benefit pension plans, which guaranteed participants a specified monthly income for the duration of their retirement years, have been quickly disappearing. In addition, there are fewer workers paying into Social Security now due to the shift in our aging population, which puts a tremendous amount of strain on the income benefits.

Coupled with all this uncertainty comes a vast amount of risk. Even for those who are good savers and investors, there are areas that must be planned for and protected so that all those years of hard earned savings aren't washed down the drain.

THE PROOF IS IN THE PLANNING

In 2009, the Hartford Life Insurance Company conducted a study titled "The Hartford Investments and Retirement Survey." In it, the company aimed to come up with a better understanding of the "retirement needs, concerns, and perceptions of consumers in the United States – particularly those who are age 45 and older."

The Hartford essentially found that many people don't like to plan – at least when it comes to their retirement: "Retirement and/or financial planning is viewed as too complex or difficult by one in two Americans (50 percent). Many people (35.5 percent) say they would rather not spend more time on financial planning."

On the other hand, those who do have a retirement plan are much more likely to be confident in their ability to create a sustainable amount of retirement income and to have a more successful retirement overall: "Those who have planned for retirement are three times more likely to be confident that they will have sufficient income in retirement as compared to those who have not planned. Nearly one-third (31.5 percent) of those who had planned said that they were 'very' or 'extremely' confident of having sufficient income for retirement as compared to 10 percent of those who had not planned."

The Hartford concluded that "those who have a plan for retirement are not only in a better place financially, but also have a more positive outlook about their retirement future than those who don't have a plan." So why is it, then, that we don't plan for retirement?

WHY WE DON'T PLAN

While many people are well aware that planning for retirement is important, for one reason or another, they don't. People may have good intentions to sit down and take care of it "someday." But, weeks turn into months, and months turn into years, until one day, it's almost time to retire – but no actual planning has been done.

Why is that?

One reason the Hartford survey discovered had to do with the impact that the volatile financial markets have had on people, especially following the stock market and economic collapse of several years ago. With optimism about being able to retire still in decline today, many Americans seem to have simply given up hope of ever being able to fully leave a life of employment and live off their savings or other assets. Many people also feel the immense burden of being solely responsible for having enough retirement income to last throughout their lifetime.

Years ago, those who had the luxury of receiving a pension income essentially had no worries about how much their retirement income would be or how long it would last because 100 percent of the responsibility for providing this ongoing income fell to the employer. Today, however, many employers have replaced the safety net of defined benefit pension income in retirement with defined-contribution 401(k) plans, where the responsibility of saving enough to sustain one's ongoing retirement income is completely up to each individual employee.

Given the volatility of the stock market in recent years, many who have had the bulk of their savings invested in 401(k) plans still haven't recovered from the market downturn of 2008 and 2009. This has led many investors to a "why bother" attitude and has even led some individuals to stop saving for retirement in order to use their funds for "more pressing" financial obligations.

THE IMPORTANCE OF HAVING A RETIREMENT PLAN

Any successful endeavor absolutely has to have a strong foundation – and a strong foundation begins with a good plan.

Many people believe that they have a plan because they will collect Social Security and they are contributing to their 401(k) or they are shifting a few dollars into a personal IRA account.

While this may be a good start, it is not an actual plan. You will need to supplement the income you receive from these sources.

Because defined-benefit retirement plans are quickly disappearing, most of us won't know exactly how much income we will have from our employer-sponsored retirement plan until it's actually time to retire and, even then, depending on how the market is performing and what we opt to do with those funds, we still may not have an exact income figure.

It is also highly unlikely that your income from Social Security will cover all of your living expenses in retirement. The Social Security Administration reported that the average monthly benefit for senior citizens was $1,077 in 2011, and the payment you receive in the future will possibly be even less in actual dollars after inflation. Assuming $1,000 in monthly payments, $12,000 per year simply cannot cover all of a typical retiree's costs – and these circumstances are simply not going to improve.

It is safe to say, then, that even with the combined income from Social Security and your employer's retirement plan, there could be a considerable "gap" between the amount of income that you need and the amount of income that you will have. Having a solid retirement plan can help you fill this gap.

A plan will help ensure that your retirement income will keep pace with the rising cost of goods and services in the future. Inflation can decimate purchasing power over time. For example, if you are receiving $3,000 per month from your portfolio, the purchasing power at 4 percent inflation will be cut by more than half in 20 years and by more than two-thirds in 30 years. Even if inflation averages only 3 percent per year over the next 15 years, you will need about $4,700 per month in order to match the purchasing power of $3,000 in today's dollars. However, there have been some periods, such as the late 1970s, when inflation soared into the double digits. This can make inflation extremely problematic for retirees who are on fixed incomes.

There are other reasons to plan ahead, too, such as unexpected or uninsured long-term care expenses that can come up in the future. According to the US Department of Health and Human Services, the odds of needing long-term care for at least some period of time in our life are roughly 70 percent. Based on MetLife's Market Survey of long-term care costs, the national average rate for a private room in a skilled nursing home facility in 2012 was over $90,500 per year, with an expectation of continued rising. There aren't many portfolios that can take a $90,000 annual hit for long without having a severely negative effect.

In order to combat such risks as inflation, potential long-term care needs, and unexpected market events, you must have a plan and put that plan into motion.

CREATING THE IDEAL RETIREMENT PLAN FOR YOU

When you are developing your plan, you need to ask yourself two simple questions:

What do you NEED your retirement income to do?

What do you WANT your retirement income to do?

As surprising as it may seem, many retirees cannot confidently answer either of these questions. Luckily, the answer to the first question should be the same for all retirees: Your retirement income must cover your basic living expenses.

Looking at your current expenses, you can determine how much income you will need to pay the monthly expenses in retirement: cost of food, housing, electricity, credit card debt, cell phone, cable, medical expenses, taxes, and all the other bills that you owe every month. Especially take note of expenses that may be reduced or eliminated: meals out with your coworkers, new work clothes, commuting costs, membership fees associated with your profession, and parking expenses related to your job. Reviewing these costs will help you to use realistic assumptions in your retirement plan.

Base your income needs on your actual expenses, not on popular notions. For example, it is a popular notion that everyone must replace 80 percent of their pre-retirement income in order to sustain their lifestyle after they retire. Such assumptions can cause many Americans to feel disheartened that retirement is out of their reach.

The truth is, people retire every day and live comfortably on much less than 80 percent. There are some experts who think that you might only need 60 percent to meet your basic retirement needs. David Blanchett, the head of retirement research at Morningstar, a leading investment research firm, and the author of *Estimating the True Cost of Retirement*, writes that retirees need to replace only 50 to 60 percent of their pre-retirement incomes. One Canadian study, Statistics Canada, found that most Canadians retire on 62 percent of their working income.

The best advice I can give you is to determine how much you will need to cover your retirement income goals.

WHAT CAN HAVING A RETIREMENT PLAN GIVE YOU?

Let me tell you what I like most about having a retirement plan. Having a retirement plan gives retirees the confidence they need to truly enjoy their retirement. Over the years, I have seen many retirees deny themselves the retirement that they are entitled to because they want to make sure they have money "just in case" something happens.

I often ask people if they have done all the things they said they were going to do in retirement. They said they were going to join the country club, buy a new boat, go on a cruise, and "see the world." I ask them, "Have you done that yet?" When they answer no, I ask why not. "Because we need to keep this money, just in case."

These people are living a "just in case" retirement!

They don't touch their money for their entire retirement, and then what happens? They pass away and it goes to their kids. What do the kids do with it? They join the country club, they buy a new boat, they go on a cruise, and they see the world.

John Homer, a financial professional from Utah, has noticed that some of his most successful clients are more concerned about what inherited wealth may do "to" their children than what it may do "for" them. How people leave their wealth often says more about who they are, or were, than how they used their wealth during their lifetime. He uses a Legacy Questionnaire to determine this:

- "If you were examining your family 20 years after your passing, what must have happened in order for you to be happy with your planning? What if the examination takes place 100 years after your passing?"
- "How do you keep your net worth from poisoning your True Wealth?"
- "What is the purpose of your wealth?"
- "How do you provide tools instead of toys?"
- "How can you empower children to reach their dreams?"

- "How will you protect assets from creditors and divorce?"
- "If there were no estate tax, what would you leave to your family?"
- "Does your estate plan reinforce core values that you esteem, or does it just deal with the stuff?"
- "Will your plan encourage your children to acquire their own wealth or just consume yours? Are you pumping out too much too early?"
- "Will the date of your death become the date of your heirs' retirement?"

My friends, I don't want you to live a "just in case" retirement. Make a retirement plan. Having one will help you to stop worrying so much about retirement!

BUT WILL THE MONEY LAST?

My friend Christie Mueller is a financial professional. She designed a retirement plan that helped her mother stop worrying about retirement through a lifetime income annuity. After Christie's father passed away, Christie's mother was worried that she would not have enough money to secure her retirement. But, after running the numbers, Christie discovered that her mother would be able to live very comfortably with the income from a lifetime income annuity.

Like many retirees, Christie's mother wanted to leave a legacy to her children. Christie told her mother to instead spend her money on living expenses and to be comfortable. Even while her health was deteriorating, Christie's mother kept asking the question, "Will the money last?"
"Everything is fine, Mom," Christie would tell her, knowing that the annuity would be enough. Seeing the peace of mind in her mother's eyes was "priceless." Christie has now been able to

8

duplicate that over and over again with many of her clients.

Christie's mother passed away several years ago, but Christie is happy that her mother had a plan that helped her to enjoy her retirement while avoiding a "just in case" retirement.

THE IMPORTANCE OF WORKING WITH A FINANCIAL PROFESSIONAL

When creating your retirement plan, you could certainly go it alone. But then again, you could also try doing your own dental work, too. In either area, doing it yourself may work well for some but not so well for others. Just like anything else, the mastering of personal finance takes many hours of ongoing, consistent education and research that most people don't have the time to do. For the majority of people, retirement is not a "do it yourself" project.

When asked what or who they relied on for credible financial planning advice, an overwhelming number of respondents in the Hartford survey who did not use the advice of a financial professional stated that they did not know where to turn. Almost that same percentage of individuals was also unsure of what to do in terms of their overall approach to investing.

Financial professionals can help you tackle specific goals as well as provide you with overall advice on retirement and estate planning. This can be especially helpful if you have assets in many different places, such as an employer-sponsored retirement plan, investment accounts at a brokerage firm, accounts at a bank, and real estate investments.

Bringing everything together into one cohesive unit will help you see the big picture and weed out what isn't working by adding in alternative options that may fit your financial goals better.

ALL RESPONDENTS

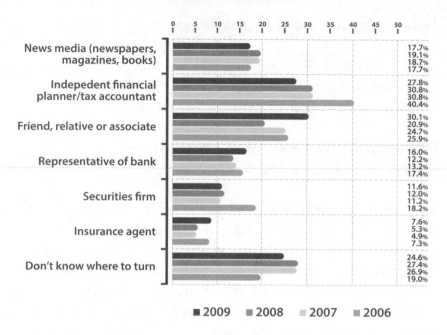

News media (newspapers, magazines, books)	17.7% / 19.1% / 18.7% / 17.7%
Indepedent financial planner/tax accountant	27.8% / 30.8% / 30.8% / 40.4%
Friend, relative or associate	30.1% / 20.9% / 24.7% / 25.9%
Representative of bank	16.0% / 12.2% / 13.2% / 17.4%
Securities firm	11.6% / 12.0% / 11.2% / 18.2%
Insurance agent	7.6% / 5.3% / 4.9% / 7.3%
Don't know where to turn	24.6% / 27.4% / 26.9% / 19.0%

■ 2009 ■ 2008 ■ 2007 ■ 2006

PLANNERS VS. NON-PLANNERS

News media (newspapers, magazines, books)	20.3% / 14.6%
Indepedent financial planner/tax accountant	39.9% / 13.4%
Friend, relative or associate	30.7% / 29.4%
Representative of bank	19.0% / 12.5%
Securities firm	16.5% / 5.7%
Insurance agent	10.2% / 4.4%
Don't know where to turn	9.6% / 42.5%

■ 2009 Created a plan ■ No plan

10

ALL RESPONDENTS

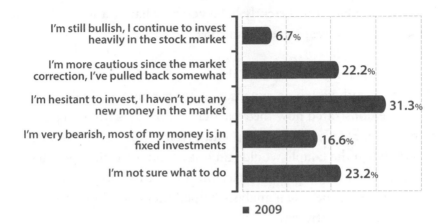

I'm still bullish, I continue to invest heavily in the stock market — 6.7%

I'm more cautious since the market correction, I've pulled back somewhat — 22.2%

I'm hesitant to invest, I haven't put any new money in the market — 31.3%

I'm very bearish, most of my money is in fixed investments — 16.6%

I'm not sure what to do — 23.2%

■ 2009

PLANNERS VS. NON-PLANNERS

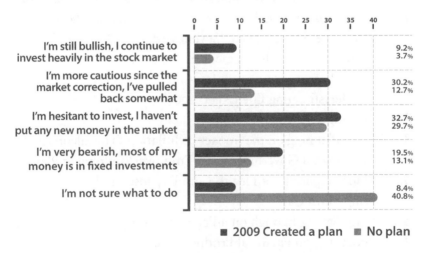

I'm still bullish, I continue to invest heavily in the stock market — 9.2% / 3.7%

I'm more cautious since the market correction, I've pulled back somewhat — 30.2% / 12.7%

I'm hesitant to invest, I haven't put any new money in the market — 32.7% / 29.7%

I'm very bearish, most of my money is in fixed investments — 19.5% / 13.1%

I'm not sure what to do — 8.4% / 40.8%

■ 2009 Created a plan ■ No plan

A financial professional can help you stay on track and remain disciplined about the strategies that you've put in place. Because procrastination is one of the biggest threats to the success of your retirement planning, having someone coach you can truly pay off.

In my book *Retirement Income Masters*, financial professional Briggs Matsko of California discussed the importance of showing people how their current plans will work out over time.

Visualizing what you currently have versus what you want will ease some peoples' unrealistic expectations.

Briggs recalled a couple from California who had dreams of a retirement with very high expenses. After running an analysis, Briggs demonstrated how their particular goal was not going to be possible. He was able to pinpoint, given certain assumptions, exactly when the couple would run out of money if they pursued that particular retirement lifestyle. Although this wasn't what they wanted to hear, the visual analysis helped them develop a more realistic financial strategy.

John Curry, a financial professional from Florida also featured in my *Retirement Income Masters* book, knows the typical mistakes that many people make. He identified "Seven Mistakes Most People Make When Preparing for Their Retirement":

1. "Underestimating Life Expectancy"
2. "Paying Too Much in Taxes"
3. "Not Planning on the Impact of Inflation (The Silent Thief)"
4. "Relying on Government and Employer Retirement Plans"
5. "Not Preparing for Health Care Expenses and Long-Term Care"
6. "Not Saving Enough on a Personal Basis"
7. "Focusing on Financial Products Instead of Strategic Planning"

To combat these mistakes, John developed Retirement Vision Questions:

1. "Think ahead to the day of your retirement. Looking back from that day, what must have happened along the way for you to feel happy about retirement?"

2. "What obstacles and concerns stand in your way to achieving your vision of retirement?"
3. "What are the most important actions that you must take in order to overcome these obstacles and concerns?"
4. "What progress have you already made toward achieving your retirement vision?"

Having a vision and a developed plan will put you – not the market – in control.

My colleague Brian Heckert, CLU, ChFC, AIF, has noticed a shift over the years. "Planning for retirement seemed to be so much simpler when the only decision an employee had to make was 'when.' And in the past, that decision was often made for the employee with a mandatory retirement date. Today, we are seeing clients come in with five to ten years left to work and they have that dazed and confused look in their eyes because of all the choices they will need to make. Choices like when they will retire, how much income do they need, where they will invest their money, how long will it last in the event of a market decline, what happens when they have a long-term care event? All of these questions must be answered, but most people do not know where to go to get their answers. Working with a knowledgeable retirement professional who has been through this before will help them answer these questions the right way and in the right order."

Brian goes on to say that the most important part of retirement planning is the plan itself. Once the plan is developed, the products that fund the plan will fall into place. If income is the most important part of the plan, products like annuities that are built for income become one of the most important parts of the plan, and the other investments can then be built around that income base.

A financial professional can transform your vision into reality. My friend Rao Garuda, a financial professional in Ohio, once met with a 65-year-old doctor from India. He asked the prospect his standard question: "If money wasn't an issue in your life, what would you do?" The doctor told Rao that his dream was to be able to send ten students to medical school in India each year for the rest of his life. By moving $100,000 to a 501(c)3 using a lifetime income annuity, Rao helped the doctor accomplish his goal.

When the time came for the client to write the check, his hands started shaking and he began to cry. Hugging Rao, the grateful client told him, "You have no idea what you have done for me."

I highly recommend that you find a financial professional whom you trust who can help you to create, implement, and regularly review *your* retirement plan, not a cookie cutter plan. This may entail some work, but it will be well worth it in the end.

FINDING THE RIGHT FINANCIAL PROFESSIONAL FOR YOU

Today, just about anyone can hang out a shingle as a financial professional – but that doesn't necessarily make that person an expert. You must do your research before you find the individual who works best for you. It is important to take into account the following points.

Reputation

Talk to your friends and co-workers – you know who the most financially successful ones are. Ask them whom they use. Get several recommendations and interview them. You will likely find one who clicks with you.

Look for someone who has been in business for more than just a few years. You want someone who is experienced and has a successful track record. I would want to find someone who specializes in retirement planning and retirement income. The successful stock broker who helped someone grow their assets may not be the one to help them take retirement income from those assets.

You want someone who really focuses on providing income (and I would argue guaranteed lifetime income) for the rest of your life and helping you manage, reduce, and even eliminate key retirement risks.

Pay Structure

One key aspect you will want to inquire about is how the financial professional is paid. Typically, financial professionals can be paid in several different ways. Two of the most common include sales commissions from products that are sold to clients and fees based on the amount of assets held.

I am less concerned about *how* someone is paid and more concerned about *why* they are recommending a certain product. Too often we hear commentators say that someone is recommending a product "just for the commissions." While this can happen, many times the product actually does solve the client's problem.

These same commentators also imply that the best investment is the one with the lowest fees. That is also wrong in many cases: I don't get to retire on "low fees." I get to retire on the products that make the most and lose the least *after* fees!

Fee-based financial professionals may have less of an incentive to sell particular products, as they are paid based on a percentage of the total assets that they manage. For example, if a fee-based professional earns 1 percent on your annual assets and you have $1 million under management with that individual, then they will earn $10,000 per year for simply managing your assets, regardless of the products you're invested in. In this case, a fee-based financial professional may be less inclined to liquidate your investments to purchase a home, for instance, or buy a lifetime income annuity, even if that is the right thing for you to do at the time, because their asset management fee would decrease.

Before moving forward with a financial professional, make sure you fully understand how that person will be paid, and try to ascertain that he or she truly cares about how you will benefit from following his or her advice.

Regulation

Financial professionals who engage in providing investment advice to others are required to be regulated on both the federal and state level. Prior to being allowed to offer any type of financial advice, these individuals must be educated on specific topics and pass certain examinations depending on the type of advice they will be offering.

Professionals who sell securities must take and pass a national securities examination. In addition, investment professionals are also required to register or become licensed in each state where they practice, pay a fee, disclose certain information, and maintain a bond or minimum amount of net capital.

If you want to run a check on any financial professional, it is easy to do so through the Financial Industry Regulatory

Authority, or FINRA. This entity maintains an online database that includes the licensing and registration information on active registered advisors across the nation. You can find details on a financial professional's employment history over the past ten years, any disciplinary history, and the status of their license and registration.

Professional Designations

In checking out financial professionals, you are also likely to run across an "alphabet soup" of industry designations. While these designations are not required for professionals to offer certain products or services, they do indicate that a person is serious about the work that they do in the financial services field.

Some of the designations you may come across will likely include:

CFP
(CERTIFIED FINANCIAL PLANNER)
– To earn the Certified Financial Planner designation, a financial professional must pass extensive examinations in the areas of financial planning, taxes, insurance, estate planning, and retirement planning. In order to maintain the CFP, regular annual continuing education courses are required.

CLU
(CHARTERED LIFE UNDERWRITER)
– The Chartered Life Underwriter designation is granted to financial professionals who complete intensive training in the areas of life insurance and personal financial planning. Course topics include insurance, investments, taxation, employee benefits, estate planning, accounting, management and economics.

CHFC
(CHARTERED FINANCIAL CONSULTANT)
– To earn the Chartered Financial Consultant designation, a professional must meet requirements in financial expertise as well as pass exams that cover finance and investing. Experience requirements include at least three years of active involvement in the financial services industry. The course exams cover topics in financial planning, income taxation, insurance, investments and estate planning.

RICP
(RETIREMENT INCOME CERTIFIED PROFESSIONAL)
– Because the thousands of Americans who are retiring every day need advice on turning their accumulated assets into income, advisors who have the RICP designation are taught how to better advise clients to do that. In order to earn the RICP, individuals are required to complete in-depth course work on retirement planning. These courses deal with asking the right questions of clients so that the best income planning approaches can be developed. Although this is a relatively new designation, having it shows that a professional truly specializes in retirement income.

Additional Information to Consider

Before making your final decision on a financial professional, you should consider these questions:

- What is the professional's track record, and do they have references that you can contact to back up these claims?
- Does the professional have any third-party references or validations such as the Chamber of Commerce or the Better Business Bureau?
- Has the professional any type of agreement that will specifically

outline or detail the services that they will provide for you?

- When you meet with the professional, does he or she really listen to your concerns?
- Is he or she aligned with a reputable and financially strong company or companies?
- Does the individual have any published materials such as a book that he or she has authored that is indicative of his or her expertise in the financial arena?
- While these may sound like tough questions, they are important to address before moving forward with someone to whom you will be entrusting your life savings. Remember, you want to be comfortable yet confident that you are working with the best financial professional possible when creating your personal plan for the future.

KEY CHAPTER POINTS

- Your retirement plan is the blueprint that will show you how to get from where you are now financially to where you want to be in the future.
- Even those who are good savers need to plan so that years of saving aren't quickly washed down the drain.
- People don't plan to fail – they simply fail to plan.
- Retirees who have retirement plans not only have a specific direction to go in, but they also feel more secure – and happier – than those without a plan.
- Many Americans seem to have given up hope of ever being able to fully leave a life of employment and live off their savings or other assets.
- Today, many people feel an immense burden of being solely responsible for having enough retirement income to last throughout their lifetime.
- Any successful endeavor absolutely has to have a strong foundation—and a strong foundation begins with a plan.

- One of the biggest reasons to have a retirement plan is to supplement the income that is received from employer-sponsored retirement plans and Social Security.
- Retirement plans must also be developed to help keep income on pace with inflation, to prepare for unexpected expenses, and to take key retirement risks off the table.
- People must know what they NEED their retirement income to do and what they WANT their retirement income to do.
- The truth is that many people can live comfortably on 70 percent or less of their pre-retirement income.
- A retirement plan can help you to stop living a "just in case" retirement.
- It is important to work with a trusted financial professional in developing a retirement plan that works for you and your specific goals.

Step 2:
Maximize Social
Security Benefits

Let me ask you a question: What is the largest retirement asset that most Americans have – their corporate pension, their 401(k), their home, or their Social Security benefit? Most people think their 401(k). The truth is that the largest retirement asset that most Americans have is actually their Social Security benefit.

Social Security was established in 1935 to alleviate poverty among the elderly during the Great Depression. Today, millions of Americans rely on Social Security, and, for many, it is their primary source of retirement income.

While most people have thought for years that the biggest purchase you will ever make is your home – and it very well may be – and that the largest amount of savings you may have could quite likely be found in your 401(k), the truth is that the largest retirement asset that most Americans have is actually their Social Security benefit.

If you are single and you've worked for 30 years, depending on how much you've contributed, your lifetime Social Security benefit could be worth more than $500,000. If you're married, your combined lifetime benefit could be worth in excess of $1 million and even more if you use certain Social Security benefit maximization strategies.

Just how big is the Social Security program? Much bigger than most people might imagine.

Every Day	• 182,000 people visit Social Security Administration field offices • 445,000 people call the Social Security Administration
in 2014	• 17 million applications for original and replacement Social Security cards will be submitted • 59 million Americans will receive Social Security benefits • $863 billion in benefits will be paid out
Overall	• 46.6 million Americans are age 65 or older • 9 out of 10 individuals are 65 or older receive Social Security benefits • 52% of coples and 74% of unmarried individuals who receive benefits get at least half of their income from Social Security • 34% of the workforce has no savings set aside specifically for retirement - Social Security benefits will help to keep these people out of poverty

Unfortunately, there are many Americans who don't take advantage of maximizing their Social Security benefits and, in the process, end up losing access to hundreds of thousands of dollars. This is why our second step to retirement security is maximizing your Social Security benefits.

The process of maximizing, or increasing, your Social Security benefit involves timing. To fully maximize your benefit, you must consider the appropriate start date to begin receiving your retirement payout so that you and your family can get the largest possible amount of lifetime income benefits.

There are also benefits that some people may never even have known existed that they are eligible for. Did you know that you can claim benefits on an ex-spouse? Or, that if you are a widow, you can claim benefits as early as age 60? In addition to maximization strategies, we will also discuss the different benefits available to you through the Social Security program that may also net you more income.

THE PROBLEM REALLY ISN'T SO BAD – OR IS IT?

Over the years, there has been a lot of discussion about the problems that the Social Security program has faced. First, there are 78 million baby boomers in America, which equates to roughly 26 percent of the population. Every last one is rushing headlong into retirement. One by one, they will stop working, stop contributing to Social Security, and begin taking money from the program. Going forward, there are going to be far fewer people paying into the system and there will be more people taking benefits out, additionally these people will be living longer.

In addition, the government will have raised the full retirement age from 65 to 67 before the year 2022. This will mean even lower Social Security benefit payments for those who take benefits at age 62. On the flip side, those who remain working until age 67 will miss out on two years of Social Security benefits that their parents received.

Payroll taxes are used to fund the Social Security program, with any surplus held in a trust fund to help cover the cost of the boomers' retirement. However, the trust fund is actually a pile of IOUs. Congress has already spent the money! Furthermore, the monthly benefit payments certainly will not be enough to cover average living expenses.

As we discussed in Step 1, at approximately $1,000 per month, the average monthly retirement benefit from Social Security isn't enough to cover most retirees' living expenses. At this time, the US government doesn't foresee any significant increases in the payments; decreases are more likely.

What can you expect from Social Security in the future? Although nobody can predict this, it's highly unlikely that the benefits will be as generous as they once were.

Two simple changes could help fix the system for the rest of our lifetimes. First, gradually raise the retirement age by one month for every two years that you are younger than age 50. For instance, my father got full Social Security at age 65. I won't get mine until age 67. Is it that unreasonable that my 12 year old daughter won't get hers until age 69 or 70? Her life expectancy will be longer than mine and my father's, after all.

The second change has to do with the way Social Security benefits are initially calculated. Currently, the initial benefits for new retirees are increased each year based on wage growth, or the rate of increase in the national average wage. However, if initial benefits were instead indexed to price growth, which measures actual purchasing power, the long-term solvency of the system would be ensured, according to a Social Security Administration report from 2010.

On average, wages tend to grow faster than prices. As a result, price-indexed initial benefits would grow more slowly than wage-indexed benefits. The downside of indexing initial benefits to price growth is that it would mean slightly lower monthly benefit levels for future retirees than what they would have received under the current plan.

Changes to the tax system may be needed as well. Currently, only $117,000 of income is taxed for Social Security. We may see this increased in the future.

Overall, though, Social Security will survive in some form. Future retirees might not get their parents' benefit amount in real (inflation-adjusted) terms, but they will receive a Social Security check in retirement and it will be greater in nominal dollars than what their parents received.

The "when" and the "how" they receive that check, however, could make a tremendous difference in its dollar amount, especially when factored in over time. Maximizing your Social Security benefits alone can make a huge difference in your retirement lifestyle.

ARE YOU COSTING YOURSELF A DIFFERENCE IN LIFESTYLE?

Many Americans give more attention to planning their annual vacation than they do to planning their retirement or selecting their Social Security start date. Mis-timing your start date could cost your household hundreds of thousands of dollars!

You initially become eligible for Social Security by working in a Social Security–covered job where you earn "credits." You essentially earn one credit per quarter of covered work, or a maximum of four credits per year. You need 40 total credits to be eligible, or "fully insured," for Social Security retirement benefits.

Although it may be estimated, the exact amount of your monthly Social Security retirement benefit isn't determined until you turn age 62, which is the earliest age at which you can start receiving these benefits. At that time, all of your annual earnings will be indexed to account for wage inflation, and your highest 35 years of earnings are averaged. If you worked less than 35 total years, the missing years will be averaged in as $0. Social Security then uses a formula to come up with your average indexed monthly earnings that will, in turn, determine your primary insurance amount, or PIA.

In the past, full retirement age was 65. Due in large part to longer life expectancy – and, therefore, longer benefit payouts – the full retirement age has been gradually increased to 67, depending on your year of birth. If you decided to apply for your benefits at age 62, the amount of your PIA would be reduced to 75 percent of its initial value because you would not have reached what Social Security deems your full retirement age.

SOCIAL SECURITY FULL RETIREMENT AGE

YEAR OF BIRTH	MINIMUM RETIREMENT AGE FOR FULL BENEFITS
1937 or Before	65
1938	65 + 2 Months
1939	65 + 4 Months
1940	65 + 6 Months
1941	65 + 8 Months
1942	65 + 10 Months
1943 to 1954	66
1955	66 + 2 Months
1956	66 + 4 Months
1957	66 + 6 Months
1958	66 + 8 Months
1959	66 + 10 Months
1960 or After	67

When you apply for your Social Security, benefits can have a lot to do, then, with how much you will receive in income per month and, in turn, with your overall retirement lifestyle.

SOCIAL SECURITY BENEFIT MAXIMIZATION STRATEGIES

Due to low savings rates, longer wait times before full retirement age, and a whole host of other factors, many people need to do whatever it takes to make the most of their retirement benefits. The Social Security benefit maximization strategies described here may be able to increase or stretch your benefit dollars.

Delaying Benefits

One easy way to increase your Social Security benefits is to simply delay their receipt past your normal retirement age. In doing so, you will earn what is referred to as delayed retirement credits.

For each year that you delay the start of your Social Security retirement benefits past your full retirement age, your benefit amount will increase by 8 percent per year up to age 70. At this point, you can still hold off on receiving your benefits, but you won't receive any additional credits for benefit increases.

For example, if your normal retirement age was 66 and your initial monthly benefit amount was $2,000 but you waited until age 70 to start receiving benefits, then your benefit amount would increase by 32 percent to $2,640, which doesn't include any annual cost of living adjustments that may also be added.

ASSUMING A FULL RETIREMENT AGE OF 66 AND A MONTHLY PIA OF $2,000

AGE	% OF FULL RETIREMENT BENEFIT	MONTHLY BENEFIT	ANNUAL BENEFIT
66	100%	$2,000	$24,000
67	108%	$2,160	$25,920
68	116%	$2,320	$27,840
69	124%	$2,480	$29,760
70	132%	$2,640	$31,680

On the other end of the spectrum, taking benefits early can significantly reduce your monthly income.

ASSUMING A FULL RETIREMENT AGE OF 66 AND A MONTHLY PIA OF $2,000

AGE	% OF FULL RETIREMENT BENEFIT	MONTHLY BENEFIT	ANNUAL BENEFIT
62	75%	$1,500	$18,000
63	80%	$1,600	$19,200
64	86.66%	$1,733	$20,798
65	93.33%	$1,867	$22,399
66	100%	$2,000	$24,000

The reduction is even harsher the higher your normal retirement age is.

ASSUMING A FULL RETIREMENT AGE OF 67 AND A MONTHLY PIA OF $2,000

AGE	% OF FULL RETIREMENT BENEFIT	MONTHLY BENEFIT	ANNUAL BENEFIT
62	70%	$1,400	$16,800
63	75%	$1,500	$18,000
64	80%	$1,600	$19,200
65	86.66%	$1,733	$20,978
66	93.33%	$1,867	$22,399
67	100%	$2,000	$24,000

The amount of income that you receive when you first begin to take your Social Security benefits will set the base for the amount that you will receive for the rest of your life, plus any annual cost-of-living adjustments. In addition, you could still receive higher Social Security benefits if you continue to work.

File and Suspend

The file and suspend technique can be used by married couples. The higher earning spouse can establish a benefit amount by applying for benefits at any time after reaching full retirement age. But, instead of actually receiving benefits, that person immediately suspends the receipt of their Social Security income until a later date.

At that time, the lower earning spouse applies for the Social Security spousal benefit of the higher earning spouse's earning record. The lower earning spouse can get one-half of the higher earning spouse's Social Security benefit. Remember, this amount will be reduced if it is taken prior to full retirement age. When the higher earning spouse turns age 70, he or she can start receiving the benefits, which will be higher due to delayed retirement credits. That higher amount will also be the survivor benefit to the surviving spouse.

For example, John is 66 but still works full time. His wife, Sarah, is a stay-at-home spouse and has never worked outside of the home. Because John has reached his full retirement age, he is able to voluntarily suspend the receipt of his benefit, allowing him to receive delayed retirement credits. Once John has applied for his benefits, Sarah—because she is over age 62—can apply for her Social Security spousal benefits, based on John's work record.

Sarah could start receiving spousal income benefits right away, while John's benefits would accrue the maximum amount of delayed retirement credit until he reaches age 70. However, if Sarah wasn't at full retirement age, her spousal benefit would be reduced. Or, if Sarah had earned a Social Security benefit on her own, she could have started her reduced benefit at age 62, taken a full spousal benefit at age 66, and then received the survivor benefit upon John's death.

The file and suspend strategy can essentially be used as a type of insurance plan. Those who file and suspend their benefits have the right to request a lump sum payment during the suspension period; doing this forfeits any delayed retirement credits that are earned during the same timeframe. This can be extremely beneficial for those who are not married and who find that they need a large amount of cash right away rather than a larger monthly benefit later.

Restricted Application Strategy

The restricted application strategy also involves using spousal benefits while allowing the higher earning spouse to earn delayed retirement credits on their benefits. This can work for Social Security benefit recipients who are married as well as certain qualifying recipients who are divorced, provided that their marriage lasted for at least ten years.

When using this strategy, an individual who has reached full retirement age will file a restricted application for spousal benefits only. Then, when that spouse turns age 70, he or she should file for his or her own benefits, which by that time will have increased to their maximum amount. Therefore, an individual can essentially collect Social Security spousal benefits while at the same time delay his or her own benefit while it collects credits.

This strategy works best for married couples or qualifying divorced couples who each have a work record and when one of the spouses will work past his or her full retirement age. It is also beneficial if the smaller full retirement benefit is greater than 50 percent of the larger full retirement benefit.

As an example, Bob and Judy recently celebrated their 66th birthdays and can start to receive their full Social Security benefits.

Judy is ready to retire and she decides to begin her Social Security benefits immediately. Bob plans to work for a few more years.

Their financial professional discusses a strategy that would permit Bob and Judy to receive benefits immediately while still allowing Bob's benefit to increase 8 percent. Judy will file for her benefits immediately at age 66. After she has filed, Bob will submit a restricted application for his spousal benefits only, meaning that he will receive 50 percent of Judy's benefit. By only filing for his spousal benefit, his own benefit will continue to grow at 8 percent per year until age 70. When Bob turns 70, he will then file and switch over to his own benefit, which will then be 32 percent higher than if he had started taking it at age 66.

It is important to note that only one spouse at a time is allowed to apply this strategy. In other words, both spouses cannot claim spousal benefits on each other's work record and then subsequently obtain delayed retirement credits on each of their own benefits.

File for Back Payments

Filing for back payments will not require having a spouse in order to maximize your benefits. If you are six months older than your full retirement age and you have not yet filed for your benefits, then you can request that your benefits begin from the time that you initially attained your full retirement age. You will essentially be allowed to receive "back pay" from the income that you had not claimed over those first six months (or longer, depending on how long you waited to file).

If you are at your full retirement age or over and you took advantage of the file and suspend strategy, you could end up receiving a large check from Social Security, depending on when you initially filed your application. This is because your original start date may be anywhere from several months to several years ago. The filing of your claim will not only trigger your back pay, but it will also begin your future Social Security benefit payments.

Spousal, Survivor, and Divorcee Benefits

The spouse of an eligible Social Security recipient does not need a work record of their own in order to claim spousal benefits. If a spouse does work, though, he or she will be eligible for the higher of two amounts – either his or her own benefit or up to 50 percent of his or her worker spouse's PIA amount, provided that the worker spouse has applied for benefits.

Similar to a worker's retirement benefits, Social Security spousal benefits can also be reduced or maximized based upon when they are received. In order to be eligible for spousal benefits, an individual must be at least age 62. If the spouse begins collecting spousal benefits prior to his or her full retirement age, the amount will be reduced to below 50 percent of the worker's PIA amount.

ASSUMING A FULL RETIREMENT AGE OF 66 AND A MONTHLY SPOUSAL BENEFIT OF $1,000

AGE	% OF FULL RETIREMENT BENEFIT	MONTHLY SPOUSAL BENEFIT	ANNUAL SPOUSAL BENEFIT
62	70%	$1,400	$16,800
62	35%	$700	$8,400
63	37.5%	$750	$9,000
64	41.7%	$834	$10,008
65	45.8%	$916	$10,992
66	50%	$1,000	$12,000

Likewise, initially taking benefits at age 62 with a full retirement age of 67 can have an even more drastic effect on the monthly benefit dollar amount that is received.

ASSUMING A FULL RETIREMENT AGE OF 67 AND A MONTHLY SPOUSAL BENEFIT OF $1,000

AGE	% OF FULL RETIREMENT BENEFIT	MONTHLY BENEFIT	ANNUAL BENEFIT
62	32.5%	$650	$7,800
63	35%	$700	$8,400
64	37.5%	$750	$9,000
65	41.7%	$834	$10,008
66	45.8%	$916	$10,992
67	50%	$1,000	$12,000

The surviving spouse of a deceased worker can also collect benefits from Social Security, provided that the worker had enough credits to qualify for Social Security retirement benefits and that the surviving spouse is age 60 or over.

In order to be eligible for Social Security survivor's benefits, a widow or widower must have been married to the deceased worker at the time of his or her death and for at least nine months prior to the worker's death. However, there are certain exceptions to the nine month rule if the worker's death is accidental or if the death occurred in the line of duty as an active member of the military.

If you and your spouse are both receiving Social Security when your spouse passes away, the deceased spouse's benefit will stop.

You can then switch over to your Social Security survivor's benefit, if it is a higher amount. Otherwise, you would maintain your own retirement benefit amount.

In determining your survivor's benefit amount, you must also consider that, when you take survivor's benefits, your own benefit will cease. Likewise, if your own benefit amount is higher and you decide to keep that one, your spouse's benefit will stop. Either way, you need to plan to keep whichever amount will be the highest going forward. Life insurance, an annuity, or some other type of additional income source should be used to help fill this gap.

In addition, if you get remarried after becoming widowed, you will no longer be eligible for Social Security survivor's benefits unless you are age 60 or over when you get remarried or are age 50 if you are disabled.

There are a few exceptions, though, where the surviving spouse may be under age 60 and still receive survivor's benefits: If the surviving spouse is caring for children under the age of 18 or if the survivor has children who are age 18 to 19 who are full-time students up to grade 12, subject to Social Security family maximum benefit amounts. The surviving spouse could also qualify to receive Social Security survivor's benefits before turning age 60 if he or she is caring for a disabled child (or children) who is (are) 18 years of age or older.

With Social Security survivor's benefits, the amount of the benefit will also be dependent on the age of the surviving spouse when they start receiving benefits. For example, if the survivor is at his or her full retirement age, then the benefit amount will be equal to the amount of the deceased worker's PIA amount. If, however, the survivor is under his or her full retirement age, then the benefit amount will be reduced by a certain percentage.

ASSUMING A FULL RETIREMENT AGE OF 67 AND A DECEASED SPOUSE'S MONTHLY BENEFIT OF $2,000

AGE	% OF DECEASED SPOUSE'S BENEFIT	MONTHLY BENEFIT	ANNUAL BENEFIT
60	71.5%	$1,430	$17,160
61	75.6%	$1,512	$18,144
62	79.6%	$1,592	$19,104
63	83.7%	$1,674	$20,088
64	87.8%	$1,756	$21,072
65	91.9%	$1,838	$22,056
66	95.9%	$1,918	$23,016
67	100%	$2,000	$24,000

While most people are aware that Social Security provides benefits for spouses and survivors, many are surprised to learn that you can also file for benefits based on a former marriage in certain situations.

Depending on how long the marriage lasted – as well as whether or not you've remarried – you could be eligible for benefits based upon your ex-spouse's work record. Collecting these benefits has no effect on your ex's benefits.

In order to qualify to collect benefits from a divorced spouse, you need to meet the following criteria:

- You were married for at least ten years.
- You are not remarried.
- The benefit that you are entitled to receive based on your own work record is less than the benefit you would receive based on your ex-spouse's work record.
- Your ex-spouse has enough credits to qualify for full Social Security retirement benefits.

Even if your ex-spouse hasn't yet applied for their Social Security retirement benefits, you can still obtain your benefits as long as your ex *qualifies* for them and you have been divorced for at least two years.

THE STATS ON WHO FILES WHEN

A recent US Government Accountability Office report highlighted who files for their benefits when; despite the fact that increased life expectancy and longer time spent in retirement can increase the potential cost of filing early, there are a large number of retirees who, for one reason or another, still file before their full retirement age.

According to the report, the large majority of workers claim benefits by the time they reach their full retirement age. Of those born in 1935, about 43 percent of men and 49 percent of women claimed benefits in the first month after turning age 62. For those born in 1946, those who claimed in the first month after turning age 62 declined to about 32 percent for men and 38 percent for women; in this group, only about 8 percent of men and 7 percent of women delayed claiming one year or more past their full retirement age.

SOCIAL SECURITY RETIREMENT INCOME CONSIDERATIONS

Despite the issues surrounding Social Security today, this program will more than likely provide you with a key component of your retirement income. Although it was never intended to replace 100 percent of an individual's pre-retirement earnings, it does give a "safety net" that, on average, replaces roughly 40 percent of an average wage earner's income after they have retired.

Unlike most other retirement sources – other than a lifetime income annuity – Social Security can provide you with a combination of benefits, including:

A SET AMOUNT OF INCOME
– While you may not have an exact figure until you file, the Social Security Administration can help you estimate what your retirement income benefit amount will be, based on your earnings history. Knowing this helps to build the rest of your retirement income plan.

LIFETIME INCOME
– Due to today's longer life expectancy, the biggest fear that most retirees have is of outliving their money. You will never outlive your Social Security income. Once you've qualified and start receiving this income, you will continue to receive it for the remainder of your lifetime, regardless of how long that may be.

COST-OF-LIVING INCREASES
– In most years, Social Security income has also been increased for inflation, which has helped retirees keep their income on pace with the rising cost of goods and services.

SURVIVOR INCOME
– Unlike many types of retirement investments—and even some pensions—Social Security pays out survivor benefits to surviving spouses as well as to other qualifying dependents.

As this chapter has proven, the income from Social Security should not be overlooked. In fact, it should be maximized whenever and wherever possible because doing so can make a real difference in your retirement income and your overall retirement lifestyle.

KEY CHAPTER POINTS

- Millions of people rely on Social Security and, for many, it is their primary source of retirement income.
- The largest retirement asset that most Americans have is their Social Security benefit.
- The process of maximizing, or increasing, your Social Security benefit involves the timing of when you will start receiving your retirement payout.
- Many Americans give more attention to planning their annual vacation than they do to planning their retirement.
- Mis-timing your Social Security benefit start date could cost your household hundreds of thousands of dollars.
- If you apply for your Social Security benefits at age 62, the amount of your benefit will be reduced to 75 percent of its initial value.
- Due to low savings rates, longer wait times before full retirement age, and a whole host of other factors, many people need to do whatever it takes to make the most of their retirement benefits.
- Despite the issues surrounding Social Security today, this program will more than likely provide you with a key component of your retirement income, so maximizing these benefits whenever and wherever you can is essential.

Step 3:
Explore a Hybrid
Retirement

Today's retirees have more post-retirement career options than any other previous generation. With the rise of Internet technology, 21st-century retirees have business opportunities available to them that retirees in the past never had, along with the ability to work from the comfort of their own homes.

In Step 3, we take a look at exploring a "hybrid" retirement. A hybrid retirement occurs when a retiree finds a full- or part-time position after leaving their primary career. They could start a small business or consult in the industry where they had built their career. Many of these retirees are excited to find an alternative position that enables them to capitalize on their experience. Today, many retirees are using a hybrid retirement in order to supplement their retirement income. In fact, seven out of ten pre-retirees expect to work well into their retirement years.

THE BENEFITS OF A HYBRID RETIREMENT

Some baby boomers have chosen a hybrid retirement because they want to, while others have gone this route because they haven't saved enough to fully live off their investments or retirement income. In either case, deciding to stay in the workforce can be financially advantageous.

A recent study by the Congressional Budget Office illustrated the impact that working just a few additional years can have on your ability to maintain your lifestyle. Each additional year that a person works can provide opportunities for increased earnings,

increased savings, and increased Social Security benefits.
A 2006 study conducted by the Urban Institute found that the additional income from post-retirement work actually paid dividends throughout one's entire retirement, not just during the time that the money was earned. Working an additional five years can boost retirement income by 56 percent.

A hybrid retirement can also offer a "middle ground" between full retirement and full-time work. Take, for instance, a client couple of my friend Christie Mueller. The husband had been laid off from the well-paying job where he had spent the bulk of his career. Initially, his goal was to find a new job in a similar capacity, work for four or five years, and then retire. But his job search became tedious and frustrating. Given the poor economy of several years ago and his advancing age, the husband wasn't having much luck. The frustration was creating both financial stress and stress in the couple's marriage.

After running an analysis for them, Christie discovered that, in order to achieve their financial goals, the couple could purchase an income annuity and the husband would only need to work part time for a few more years before fully retiring. As she explained this, she could see the relief on both of their faces.

As another example, let's consider two friends of mine, Bill and Briana Boomer, who are both age 65. They remember hearing the late comedian George Burns saying, "Retirement at sixty-five is ridiculous. When I was sixty-five, I still had pimples." George Burns lived to be age 100! So, Bill and Briana decide to enjoy a hybrid retirement for a few years. Briana accepts a position working part time at a department store, while Bill, after a full career in manufacturing, discovers that companies will pay him for his expertise.

Working at home as a consultant, Bill can bring in occasional income

– with no "heavy lifting"! Any time that Bill spends doing this is on his own schedule, and only as much as he wants. He still feels retired, but it keeps him engaged.

Besides a hybrid retirement being financially beneficial, brain scientists are adamant about how important it is to be stimulated and connected to the outside world in order to retain brain fitness. Using the experiences from retirees' careers can ultimately add more income and healthy activity to retirement happiness.

Bill and Briana are using experience from their lifetime careers to add more income and healthy activity to their retirement happiness.

REASONS RETIREES WORK IN RETIREMENT

According to the Employee Benefit Research Institute's 2014 Retirement Confidence Survey, 65 percent of workers now plan to work for pay for at least some period of time in retirement. Nearly all of the retirees who worked for pay in the survey gave a positive reason for doing so: They wanted to remain active and involved or they simply enjoyed working. There were some financial reasons, too: They wanted money to purchase "extras"; they needed money to make ends meet; they experienced a decrease in the value of their savings or investments; or they needed work to keep health insurance or other benefits.

The study also made an interesting discovery regarding both individuals who had expected to work for pay in retirement and those who actually did end up working for pay in retirement after leaving their full-time employment. Some individuals found themselves having to retire unexpectedly due to downsizing or the closing of their company. Others had to leave early due to a disability that prevented them from being able to perform the duties of their job.

REASONS FOR WORKING IN RETIREMENT, AMONG RETIREES WHO WORKED IN RETIREMENT

Is... a major reason, minor reason, or not a reason why you worked for after you retired? (2014 Retirees who have worked for pay n=149)

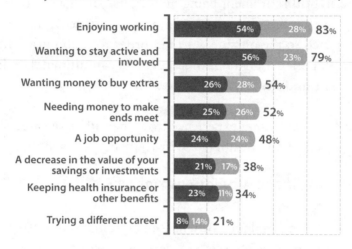

	Major reason	Minor reason	Total
Enjoying working	54%	28%	83%
Wanting to stay active and involved	56%	23%	79%
Wanting money to buy extras	26%	28%	54%
Needing money to make ends meet	25%	26%	52%
A job opportunity	24%	24%	48%
A decrease in the value of your savings or investments	21%	17%	38%
Keeping health insurance or other benefits	23%	11%	34%
Trying a different career	8%	14%	21%

■ Major reason ■ Minor reason

Approximately 26 percent found that they were able to afford retiring earlier than they had originally anticipated.

Regardless of the reason for early retirement, the overall consequences can be harsh. Those who retire earlier than planned are more likely to be less confident about having enough money for a comfortable retirement, even when it comes to basic living expenses, and especially for medical or potentially high long-term care expenses.

TURNING A HOBBY INTO CASH FLOW

Retirees today have the opportunity to turn former hobbies into incoming cash flow, whether for additional income purposes or simply for enjoyment. Because many individuals may be coming from a more structured employment environment, they can gain

COMPARISON OF EXPECTED (WORKERS EXPECTING TO RETIRE) AND ACTUAL (RETIREES) WORK FOR PAY IN RETIREMENT

Do you think you will do any work for pay after you retire?/Have you worked for pay since you retired? (2014 Workers expecting to retire n=911, Retirees n=501)

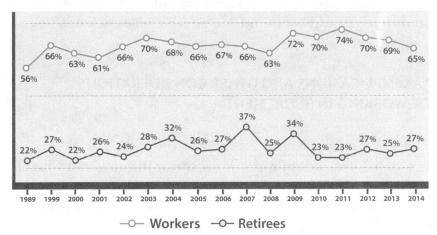

—○— Workers —○— Retirees

important business skills and knowledge through resources like AARP and the Small Business Administration.

According to a recent AARP survey, nearly one-quarter of those who are self-employed (including small business owners) are age 60 and older. Another AARP survey discovered that 10 percent of wage earners planned to start a business after they retired.

The Ewing Marion Kauffman Foundation found that "retirement-age people are starting businesses at the fastest clip of any age group": 55- to 64-year-olds accounted for 23 percent of businesses started by entrepreneurs, which was higher than the 20- to 34-year-old age group and up from 14 percent in 1996.

The seamstress from Wisconsin can now start a business in weather-resistant porch shades; the retiree with loves of decorating and weddings can have a wedding planning service; and the adventurous types can sell their house and travel in an RV, running a website part time and earning affiliate commissions from products they sell online.

By living the way that they do, these retirees can live on their own schedule, go where they want to go, and still earn part-time income on their terms, without the need to punch a time clock or answer to a supervisor.

TAX IMPLICATIONS AND OTHER CONSIDERATIONS OF WORKING IN RETIREMENT

Although working in retirement may be therapeutic or may be needed to fill an income gap, it is important to not "shoot yourself in the foot." You do not want to earn too much money and have it affect your Social Security benefits, especially if you haven't reached your full retirement age yet. This is called the Social Security earnings limit.

Here's how it works: In 2014, the annual earnings limit was $15,480, meaning that you could earn up to that amount of money without your Social Security benefits being affected. If, however, you earn more than that amount, your Social Security retirement benefits will be reduced by a certain amount, depending on your age. If you are younger than your full retirement age throughout the entire year, then Social Security will deduct $1 from your benefits for every $2 that you earn above the $15,480 earnings limit. But if you reach your full retirement age in 2014, then Social Security will deduct $1 from your benefits for every $3 that you earn above $41,400 until the month in which you reach your full retirement age.

For example, pretend you are age 62 in January 2014 and will receive $600 per month in Social Security benefits, equating to $7,200 in total annual benefits. During the year, you plan to earn $20,800.

This amount is $5,320 over the earnings limit of $15,480 for 2014. Therefore, Social Security will deduct $1 for every $2 that you earn over the limit – because you earned $5,320 over the earnings limit, Social Security will withhold $2,660 in benefits.

If you think you are going to earn over the $15,480 limit, you may want to delay taking Social Security benefits. Even if you decide to take your benefits early and continue to work, the money that Social Security "takes back" is not gone! It will be added back into your future calculations and will actually cause your future Social Security benefits to increase.

The good news is that there is no adverse effect on your Social Security retirement benefits as a result of income you earn after you reach full retirement age.

What Counts and What Doesn't Count as Income

When working in retirement, you must understand what counts and what doesn't count as actual income for the Social Security earnings limits. According to Social Security, if you work for someone else as an employee, only your wages will count toward the Social Security earnings limits. If you are self-employed, only your net self-employment earnings are counted.

Income from government benefits other than Social Security are not counted toward the Social Security earnings limits, nor are interest, investment earnings, pensions, capital gains, or annuity income. But these other forms of income *are* counted in the TAXATION of Social Security benefits. Social Security does count the contribution by you, the employee, to a pension or retirement plan if that contribution amount will be included in your gross wages for the year.

You also should be aware of when income will (or won't) be counted. If you work for wages for an employer, your income will be counted by Social Security when it is actually earned versus when it is paid to you. For those who are self-employed, your income will count when you receive it, unless the income is paid to you in a year after you become entitled to Social Security benefits but is earned before you were entitled.

Since not everyone retires on December 31st, there is a rule for the first year that you retire. Because some people who retire mid-year will have already earned more than the Social Security annual earnings limit, you are allowed to receive a full Social Security check for any whole month in which you are retired, regardless of your annual earnings.

THE EFFECT OF INCOME ON SOCIAL SECURITY RETIREMENT BENEFITS

YEARS BEFORE REACHING FULL RETIREMENT AGE	IN THE YEAR YOU REACH FULL RETIREMENT AGE	AFTER YOU REACH FULL RETIREMENT AGE
$1 is withheld from benefits for every $2 that is earned above the annual earnings limit	$1 is withheld from benefits for every $3 that is earned over the limit Only applies to earnings for months prior to turning full retirement age	No limit on earnings You receive credit for the earnings, which may increase your Social Security benefits in the future

Working in Retirement, Income Taxes, and Social Security Benefits

If you have wages from a job, self-employment income, or another type of income in retirement on top of your Social Security benefits, you will need to be careful of the potential tax implications.

Although nobody is required to pay federal income tax on more than 85 percent of their Social Security income, any taxation on your benefits takes cash out of your pocket that could be used for living expenses.

The amount of tax is based upon your household's combined income as well as the way in which your tax return is filed. Your combined income is calculated as follows:

YOUR ADJUSTED GROSS INCOME
+
NONTAXABLE INTEREST
+
1/2 OF YOUR SOCIAL SECURITY BENEFITS
=
YOUR COMBINED INCOME

Once your combined income has been determined, you can calculate the amount of your Social Security income that will be taxable, if any, based on how you file your annual tax return.

For example, if you file your federal tax return as an individual and your combined income is between $25,000 and $34,000 (in 2014), then you may be required to pay income tax on up to 50 percent of your Social Security benefits. If your combined income is over $34,000, then up to 85 percent of your Social Security benefits could be taxable. If you file a joint tax return and you and your spouse have a combined income between $32,000 and $44,000, then you may be required to pay tax on up to 50 percent of your Social Security benefits. If your combined income is in excess of $44,000, you may be taxed on up to 85 percent of your benefits.

NO SOCIAL SECURITY BENEFITS ARE TAXED IF:

YOU FILE YOUR TAXES AS:	YOU EARN
Single	Less than $25,000
Married - Filing Jointly	Less than $32,000

UP TO 50% OF YOUR SOCIAL SECURITY BENEFITS MAY BE TAXED IF:

YOU FILE YOUR TAXES AS:	YOU EARN
Single	$25,000 - $34,000
Married - Filing Jointly	$32,000 - $44,000

UP TO 85% OF YOUR SOCIAL SECURITY BENEFITS MAY BE TAXED IF:

YOU FILE YOUR TAXES AS:	YOU EARN
Single	More than $34,000
Married - Filing Jointly	More than $44,000

THE BOTTOM LINE ON EXPLORING A HYBRID RETIREMENT

All situations are different, so only you will know what will work best for you. With longer life expectancies and more active lifestyles for seniors becoming the norm, more and more retirees are choosing to turn their "retirement" into a time of exploration. Starting a new business, a new career, or a hobby-turned-to-incoming-cash-flow can be beneficial for both your current and your future income.

KEY CHAPTER POINTS

- Today's 21st-century retirees have more post-retirement career options than any previous generation.
- A hybrid retirement occurs when a retiree finds a full- or part-time position after leaving their primary career.
- Seven out of ten pre-retirees expect to work well into their retirement years.
- Each additional year that a person works can provide opportunities for increased earnings, increased savings, and increased Social Security benefits.
- Retirement-age people are starting businesses at the fastest clip of any age group.
- Earning "too much" money in retirement – primarily before you reach your full retirement age – can affect your Social Security benefits due to the Social Security earnings limit.
- It pays to discover potential income opportunities from a former hobby. It could provide an enjoyable way to spend time in retirement while also adding to incoming cash flow both now and in the future.
- Understanding how Social Security benefits are taxed can potentially save you thousands of dollars per year!

Step 4:
Protect Your Savings
from Inflation

Inflation has always been an important factor in retirement planning, but it has become even more essential as life expectancy has lengthened. Income must last for longer life spans, and the inflation problem is compounded over time. If you retire at age 65 and drop dead at age 68, inflation won't impact your retirement. However, if you live to be 85 or 90, inflation will have likely cut your purchasing power by 50 to 75 percent! That is why Step 4 is about protecting your savings from this risk.

When the government prints more dollars like it did in the recession of 2008, the value of the other dollars go down. Subsequently, when you go to buy something, you will need more dollars. This is inflation.

However, the government's act of printing money isn't the only cause of inflation. The money that is printed has to make its way into the economy in order to have any impact. This is called the velocity of money. It is a measurement of how fast money turns over in the economy based on the amount of economic activity.

Inflation will almost certainly affect everyone's retirement. It can increase the risk of running out of money, especially for retirees who are on fixed incomes and who are depending on their retirement savings to make ends meet. Inflation is the ever-rising cost of living, and it can be your worst retirement income nightmare because it will erode away your future purchasing power.

For example, at 4 percent inflation, you will need $1,000 to purchase just $500 worth of today's goods in 20 years—it will cut your purchasing power in half in 20 years. In order to safeguard your savings from inflation, you must talk to your financial professional about investment options that can beat inflation. These investments include stocks, real estate, mutual funds, and Treasury Inflation-Protected Securities, or TIPS bonds. Today, many savvy investors use mutual funds and TIPS bonds to safeguard their retirement savings from inflation.

WHAT EXACTLY IS A MUTUAL FUND?

Mutual funds allow investors to essentially "pool" their money into one professionally managed investment. These financial vehicles invest in a portfolio of stocks, bonds, commodities, and cash—or sometimes all of the above.

A mutual fund is like a big "basket" of investments. Each basket holds dozens to hundreds of investment securities. When an investor buys a mutual fund, he or she is actually buying shares, or a part of a basket of investment shares.

The advantages of mutual funds include simplicity, diversification, asset allocation, and professional asset management. With just a few dollars per month, an investor can open a mutual fund account. There are many financial professionals who think that having a diversified mix of mutual funds is a good way to beat inflation over the long haul.

THE IMPORTANCE OF PAYING YOURSELF FIRST

Regularly adding to your savings is an important step to securing your retirement – remember to PAY YOURSELF FIRST.

Most financial professionals will recommend saving 15 percent of your after-tax income for retirement. If you are thinking,

"There is no way I can put aside 15 percent of my paycheck," the good news is that you may get some help. The 15 percent figure includes any contributions that are made to your retirement account by your employer. Your retirement savings may also get help from compound interest or market appreciation; it may also be tax deferred.

Savvy savers have been able to save even more than 15 percent of their income in other ways, too. For example, you could do things such as:

- Save part of your tax refund
- Save part of your pay raise or bonus
- Save a portion of income earned from a part-time job
- Identify and eliminate unnecessary expenses

Many people will have their savings automatically deducted from their pay and deposited into their personal retirement accounts. Automatically saving money every month is a cornerstone to building wealth.

WHY INFLATION IS ESPECIALLY PROBLEMATIC FOR RETIREES

Simply setting aside money is only one step to building wealth. Wealth can be quickly eroded away by inflation, unless you are able to "hedge" that inflation using various investment methods.

Between 1982 and 2011, the presumed average inflation rate for people age 62 and over was 3.1 percent. The impact of inflation had caused a retiree's living expenses of $50,000 in 1982 to go up to $121,400 by 2011. This represents a 143 percent increase over a 29-year period of time, and it compares with a 131 percent increase for the consumer price index for the urban population, or CPI-U.

Just as inflation can change from one country to another, it can also vary among different types of goods and services that are purchased in an economy. One of the biggest reasons for the inflationary effect on seniors is the increasing cost of medical care, which has doubled compared with the overall CPI-U.

While inflation has an effect on retirement income by increasing the future costs of goods and services overall, even a relatively low rate of inflation can have a substantial impact on purchasing power for a retiree.

WHAT INFLATION LOOKS LIKE

Let's pretend that you are currently 50 years old and you will plan to retire at age 65, with a projected life expectancy of 85 years old. You currently earn $75,000 per year, and you are projecting that you will need to replace roughly 70 percent of your current income in order to pay your living expenses in retirement. You also project inflation at 3 percent. If you were to retire today, your income needs would be only $52,500, or 70 percent of $75,000.

At the assumed rate of inflation, your annual retirement income needs would increase over time, eventually reaching $147,728 at the end of your life expectancy, just for you to maintain the same standard of living that you have today. The amount of money you will need in 35 years will be nearly triple the amount that you need today just to keep pace with your same standard of living.

Now let's say that you were to live to age 95 instead. In order to keep up with your same standard of living for these additional ten

RETIREMENT INCOME NEEDS

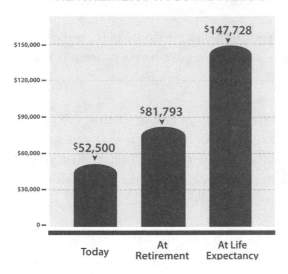

years, you will now need to be earning $198,534 per year by the end of your life expectancy just to maintain the same lifestyle that $75,000 per year is buying you today. This is nearly four times the amount of today's dollars.

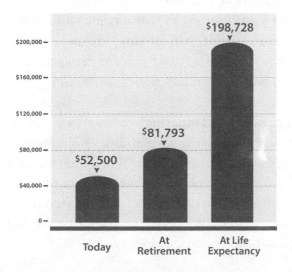

PROTECTING RETIREMENT INCOME AGAINST INFLATION

When setting up your retirement income plan, there are certain retirement income sources that are better protected against inflation than others.

For instance, if you work for an employer that still offers a defined benefit pension plan, the benefits that you will receive are oftentimes tied to the average of your three highest years of salary. Therefore, the longer you work – and the higher your salary – the higher your pension income would be.

Social Security income will typically offer a yearly cost-of-living adjustment, or COLA. This increase is based on the previous year's Consumer Price Index (CPI), which helps your Social Security income keep up with rising inflation. As discussed in Step 2, you can also help to increase your Social Security income by delaying your benefits as long as possible (up to age 70) and obtaining delayed retirement credits.

There are various retirement income products that allow you to add inflation protection options so that income will rise over time. Many annuities, for example, will let you purchase either a set amount of benefit increase, such as 5 percent per year, or an amount of increase that is based off an index such as the CPI.

You could also consider a "laddering" strategy with annuity income. This entails purchasing several different annuities that will start paying out at different times. When interest rates are low, it doesn't make sense to lock in that low rate for an extended period of time. Since no one can predict where interest rates are going in the future, purchasing annuities over a period of time can allow you to minimize your risk of low return.

For example, this is what I have personally done. I have guaranteed lifetime income that will start at age 60 with more starting at age 65, age 70, and even more at age 75. With these, I have ensured that I will have increasing income for the rest of my life. I have also purchased some of these with 3 percent annual increases. Despite the fact that I believe our economy will face deflationary pressures, I have protected myself from inflation. If it turns out that inflation is not a factor, I will have even more money to enjoy in retirement!

If you own certain types of insurance, such as long-term care, you can oftentimes add an inflation-adjusted increase to your benefits so that they, too, will increase over time. This can be a smart addition to your policy, especially if you've purchased the coverage at a younger age and may not need the benefits for a number of years.

Although bonds have lately been at historical lows, the government does offer TIPS (Treasury Inflation-Protected Securities) to help combat inflation. These are actually CPI-adjusted bonds that are purchased directly from the US government and are designed to keep pace with inflation by having their par value rise with inflation, as measured by the Consumer Price Index. Because they are purchased directly through the government, investors can avoid hefty management fees that eat into your retirement income or your return.

Another option to combat inflation in retirement is I Bonds, which are inflation-linked savings bonds. They are similar to regular savings bonds except that they offer investors inflationary protection, as their yields are tied to the inflation rate. They also have some tax advantages; therefore, they can provide a more attractive after-tax return and are virtually risk free. However, the government limits the amount of I Bonds that individuals may purchase.

If you had a bad experience in the volatile stock market several years back, you may initially shy away from equities to avoid more investment-related losses. But you should still consider having at least a certain percentage of your portfolio in financial products that have the potential for increasing returns to beat inflation. Even in periods of high inflation, equities can perform better than bonds when it comes to protecting investors against inflationary pressures. Equities don't just have to be high growth stocks, either. You could consider mixing in some solid dividend-paying stocks for income, too.

There are also certain tangible assets that can be helpful in hedging against inflation. Historically, gold had been able to protect the purchasing power of the currency invested in it. It had often been used by investors as an inflationary hedge because when the cost of living goes up, so does the price of gold. Adding gold and precious metals to a portfolio was a good way to add diversification. Unfortunately, the price of gold today is becoming much more speculative than it has been in years past. This is due in large part to traders and fund managers making bets, with very little attention to the more traditional role that gold has played in the past.

A better long-term hedge against inflation in terms of tangible assets would be to own rental real estate. Because the cost to rent is essentially incorporated into the Consumer Price Index, if the CPI increases, rents will, likely, in turn go up. This type of investment can work very well, provided that your property taxes and cost of maintenance don't increase by more than the cost of inflation and that your mortgage payments remain fixed.

THE BOTTOM LINE ON INFLATION

The risk of inflation and the loss of purchasing power is a very serious issue for those in retirement and those approaching this stage of their lives. With that in mind, it is essential to plan for both the short- and the long-term effects.

Because most people can plan to be in retirement for 20 years or more, it is important to consider the effect that inflation will have on your anticipated living expenses over time and then to plan accordingly using the proper mix of investment and protection vehicles.

KEY CHAPTER POINTS

- Inflation has always been an important factor in retirement planning, but it has become even more essential as life expectancy has lengthened. This is because a retiree's income has to last that much longer into the future.
- Inflation can increase the risk that you will run out of money in retirement by eroding away your future purchasing power.
- At 4 percent inflation, you will need $1,000 to purchase just $500 worth of today's goods in 20 years.
- It is essential to pay yourself first.
- Most financial professionals will recommend saving 15 percent of your after-tax income for retirement.
- One reason why inflation is especially problematic for retirees is due to the increasing cost of medical care.
- When setting up your retirement income plan, there are certain income sources that are better protected against inflation than others.

Step 5:
Secure More Guaranteed Lifetime Income

Guaranteed lifetime income can make or break the type of lifestyle you have in retirement along with the type of life you lead throughout that time. It can mean living where you want to live, going where you want to go, and doing what you want to do, instead of being constantly worried about spending a few too many dollars and running out of money.

My friend and colleague Dick Austin describes this difference between having and not having guaranteed lifetime income through a story about a drive in the desert. A group of Northeasterners always wanted to visit the desert, so they fly to Death Valley, California. Although the temperature was 127 degrees Fahrenheit, they rented a Lincoln Continental with ice cold air conditioning.

As they begin, the day is beautiful and the occupants chatter about the wonderful scenery, the nice, warm sunshine, and the great time that is being had by all. After a while, someone notices that the gas tank is almost on "E" and the next gas station is not for another 100 miles. No longer does the scenery matter. The previously "nice, warm sunshine" becomes uncomfortable as the occupants turn off the car's A/C and roll down the windows in the hope of saving fuel. The remainder of the trip is spent with a constant fixation on the fuel gauge. Arguments begin about how fast they should drive and what they will do if they run out of gas in the middle of the desert.

The way Dick explains it is that everyone thinks running out of money is about the *day* you run out of money, when, in fact, it is really about the years prior to that, when you know that you're going to.

Not having guaranteed lifetime income will force you to constantly look at the gas gauge, or your bank account, knowing that it will eventually get to "E" but never knowing exactly when.

In 2012, *TIME* magazine published an article entitled "Lifetime Income Stream Key to Retirement Happiness." Reporting on Britain's first-ever national happiness survey, the journalist wrote that the happiest people were those who had sources of guaranteed lifetime income. He concluded, "Securing at least a base level of lifetime income should be every retiree's priority – at least if they want to live happily ever after."

ACCUMULATING RETIREMENT SAVINGS IS THE "EASY" PART

Accumulating money is an important first step on the road to retirement. My advice is to start early by putting 15 percent of your income into a retirement savings account like an IRA, Roth, or 401(k). As you approach retirement, you should bump that up to 25 percent.

The longer you wait, the more you will have to play catch up. Recent data from the US Census Bureau indicates that salaries tend to plateau by your early forties. From that point on, it is likely that you will not receive much beyond a cost-of-living adjustment. In a worst-case scenario, if you lose a job in your fifties, it can be difficult to find another one at your equivalent salary. Given these facts, you need to save for retirement as early as possible.

As you approach retirement, you may notice that you fixate more and more on wealth accumulation. But accumulating wealth is really just a small part of the overall equation at this stage in the game.

With more and more baby boomers approaching retirement, it seems like we see more ads for various retirement savings plans from brokers, mutual fund companies and financial planning firms. The problem with most of these ads is that they focus only on the accumulation phase, the time when you are working and saving money for your retirement. They offer you a plethora of investment options and strategies along with hypothetical growth rates on your principal. They will typically make an educated estimate of how much you'll need to have accumulated by the time you retire, which they call your "magic number."

But many of these ads don't stress what you need to do with these accumulated savings once you hit retirement. After all those years of saving a percentage of your income and squirreling away funds for the future, the real goal, after all, is to convert those funds into a livable, ongoing income for your retirement. Many of the big financial companies haven't yet placed a great deal of focus on this stage.

On the day that you retire, all the rules change! You are now spending assets rather than accumulating them. Even if you save up to your accumulation goal, or your "magic number," you still run the risk of squandering it all away in poor investments or of withdrawing it too quickly.

The truth is, there is no "magic number." The accumulation phase is only the end of the beginning. The distributions from your savings have absolutely, positively got to last until the end.

HOW TO ENSURE THAT YOU DON'T RUN OUT OF MONEY BEFORE YOU RUN OUT OF TIME

Distributing assets to ensure that you get the most out of your retirement without running out of money is a difficult balancing act. Quite frankly, it should be taken even more seriously than the accumulation phase.

That being said, there are some retirees who never do anything for enjoyment during their retirement. Why? Because they are so afraid of losing money that they invest in low-yielding investments, such as passbook savings accounts or low-interest Certificates of Deposit (or as I jokingly say, Certificates of Depreciation, given today's low interest rates). Others may invest more wisely but still won't spend a nickel for fear of running out of funds.

On the other end of the spectrum are those who spend wildly during the early years of retirement, only to find out that their spending – along with the never-ending curse of inflation—has relegated them to near-poverty levels for the rest of their years.

Making withdrawals from your savings too early can have disastrous consequences on your retirement portfolio, as can taking out too much. In 2008, MetLife did a study that said 43 percent of all baby boomers believe that they can take out 10 percent per year or more from their savings once they have retired. You could do that, but you're going to run out of money very quickly! What do you think is a safe number in terms of a withdrawal percentage from your portfolio? If you think it is 5 percent, that number is still too high. Even a 4 percent withdrawal rate, a rate that was considered safe for many years, is no longer safe.

What is the safe rate now? Morningstar, an independent investment analysis firm, says that the right number is 2.8 percent. That means that if you want $28,000 of retirement income, you will need $1,000,000! In 2007, the *Wall Street Journal* published an article that explained the bulletproof withdrawal rate for a diversified portfolio: 2 percent.

When planning for your golden years, you need to think less about how much money you have saved and more about how you will spread out what you have so that it will last for the rest of your life.

SOURCES OF GUARANTEED LIFETIME INCOME

There are several sources of guaranteed lifetime retirement income: Social Security benefits, pension benefits, and annuity payouts.

Although there are many issues plaguing the Social Security program, it is highly likely that you will receive benefits from Social Security in retirement. However, you shouldn't count on this income to replace much more than one-third of your pre-retirement income. In addition, you will not see much inflation protection with this stream.

The next source of guaranteed income is the corporate pension. Although many major corporations are eliminating their traditional pension plans each year, there are millions of Americans who still have them. For those who are fortunate enough to be a participant in a defined-benefit pension plan, your employer will pay you a specified amount of retirement income for life. The responsibility for this income is solely up to the employer, not you. Typically, these benefits are paid out in the form of an annuity. Pension plans usually allow joint distributions, too, so that a surviving spouse can continue to receive retirement income benefits, which are usually 50 percent of the original income payment.

If you do happen to have a pension plan, review your documents while developing your retirement plan in order to make sure that you understand exactly what it is that you have. Today, the average monthly corporate benefit plan may not be enough to cover your basic living expenses.

Unfortunately, there are many Americans who won't receive a retirement benefit at all from their employer. For people in this situation, having a lifetime annuity is a viable way to secure a lifetime retirement income. For those who do receive a pension, an annuity can be a great way to supplement that income.

In many ways, a lifetime income annuity can be considered a "personal pension-like stream of guaranteed lifetime income." These financial vehicles can provide you with a guaranteed paycheck for life.

HOW LIFETIME INCOME ANNUITIES WORK

There are many different types of annuities in the marketplace today, but I prefer the lifetime income annuity. In exchange for a lump sum deposit, the annuity provider, such as an insurance company, will make a series of future income payments to the buyer. Often, the annuity's income payout stream can begin the month following the deposit and can last for just one person's lifetime, for two people's lifetimes, or for a certain number of years. There are a number of different ways that you can set up the payment, depending on your situation and specific income needs.

For example, let's say that a 75-year-old man purchased a lifetime income annuity and deposited $50,000 with a guaranteed payout rate of 6.56 percent for life with 20-year certain. This means that he will be guaranteed $3,280 per year, paid out in monthly installments, for the rest of his life. If he passes away prematurely, his family would continue to receive that income check for the rest of the 20-year income period. If the man lives, he will continue to receive checks for the remainder of his life, even if he lives beyond the 20-year period.

The amount of monthly check you will receive from this annuity will be dependent upon your age, gender, and the amount that you've deposited into the annuity.

For example, assuming the current interest rates and an initial deposit of $100,000, at age 65, a lifetime income annuity can guarantee a 7.10 percent payout rate for the rest of your life or a 6.45 percent rate if you want the initial premium returned to your family if you die prematurely.

At age 85, you would be guaranteed a 14.47 percent payout rate for the rest of your life or 10.46 percent if you want the guarantee for your family.

HOW LIFETIME INCOME ANNUITIES CAN MAKE SUCH HIGH GUARANTEED INCOME PAYOUTS

You may now be looking at the high payout rates on lifetime income annuities, comparing them with what you can get in today's market from other traditional retirement income products like CDs or bonds, and wondering how these products can provide this type of payout. They can do this because their payments essentially come from three sources: principal, interest, and longevity credits.

Longevity credits, also known as mortality credits, are like a longevity "bonus" for living longer. Lifetime income annuities are the only financial product I know of that are structured to satisfy the needs of aging clients, which is why the longer you wait to start your income stream, the higher your payments will be. When you add it all together, then, with these types of annuities, the older you are, the longer you live, and the fewer guarantees you take, the more longevity credits you receive.

To be clear, these credits have nothing to do with actual interest rate returns. They are an actuarial calculation by the insurance company that is based on your age and gender that adds a credit from the entire risk pool of everyone who buys the same type of lifetime income annuity.

Life insurance companies know when people are going to die. Although they don't know exactly when *you* are going to die, they do know almost exactly how long 100 people just like you will live as a group. The insurance company can pay each person as though they know when each person is going to die. Because some people will die early and will not collect income for very long, the insurance company can pay the entire pool of people a little more than a traditional investment can.

While some people may think if they buy an annuity and die prematurely that the insurance company will keep the rest of their money, this is not true. You can pick different guaranteed options to make sure that your money doesn't disappear when you die.
In fact, 92 percent of annuity buyers want a guarantee: joint life with their spouse or child or a cash refund guarantee.

CONSIDERATIONS WHEN SHOPPING FOR LIFETIME INCOME

Lifetime income annuities deliver higher payouts because, in addition to distribution gains and principal, they subsidize those who die late with the capital of those who die early.

MALE AGE 65, $100,000 INVESTMENT

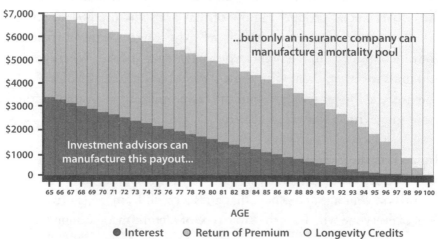

AGE

● Interest   ○ Return of Premium   ○ Longevity Credits

CONSIDERATIONS WHEN SHOPPING FOR LIFETIME INCOME

In addition to your age and gender, annuity payout rates will vary by insurer—sometimes by as much as 5 to 10 percent. Before deciding on an annuity, you will want to confirm the current payout rates with your financial professional or by checking with one of the prominent online annuity rate sources. You should also talk with your financial professional about any additional guarantees that can continue the income payments to your spouse and other loved ones should something happen to you.

When you purchase a lifetime income annuity, you are linking a portion of your retirement income to the credit worthiness of the issuing insurance company. For this reason, you must research the financial standing of your annuity provider. After all, you want the annuity to be there when you need the income stream. You can typically get a good idea of how financially stable an insurance company is and how well the company has done in paying out its claims by checking the ratings by A.M. Best, Standard & Poor's, Moody's, and Fitch Ratings.

For an added measure of security, you might consider spreading out your funds among different highly rated insurance companies and limiting the amount that you invest with any single insurer to the coverage limit of the life insurance guaranty association in your state. This amount has typically been $100,000 per insurance company, although in some states the amount has recently been raised to $250,000. You should be putting at least enough retirement funds into a lifetime income annuity to cover your basic living expenses. You will then be able to optimize the remainder of your savings, with a special eye on inflation protection, and use other income sources such as Social Security and any pension to cover the remainder of your retirement income needs.

By allocating a portion of your portfolio to some form of inflation-sensitive investments, you can optimize your portfolio against inflation and help ensure that income needs are met for life through a lifetime income annuity.

One strategy you may want to consider is buying annuities in different stages over several years. This can reduce the chances of committing all your money when interest rates are low, as they have been over the past few years. By phasing into annuities, you can also allow yourself more time to gauge the living expenses you will have in retirement and the amount of guaranteed income that you'll really need.

THE BOTTOM LINE ON LIFETIME INCOME ANNUITIES FOR GUARANTEED RETIREMENT INCOME

According to retirement experts, the lifetime income annuity is the one retirement solution that can help every American secure a guaranteed lifetime income. The Financial Research Corporation of Boston thinks that "no other investment vehicle can rival the income annuity for retirement security." The US Government Accountability Office concurred, stating, "Seniors should convert a portion of their savings into an income annuity to cover necessary expenses." Towers Watson also found that "among retirees with similar wealth and health characteristics, those with incomes from annuities are happiest."

Having a guaranteed stream of retirement income will give you other benefits that you may not have realized. Christie Mueller, the aforementioned financial professional in Seattle, had a retired couple with plenty of money but not a lot of income. While they were able to purchase many items outright, they were unable to qualify for a home loan because they had no regular incoming cash flow. Christie advised them to take a portion of their savings and convert it into a guaranteed lifetime income stream. Soon after doing so, the couple was easily able to qualify for a loan to refinance their home. Because of this regular guaranteed income stream, the clients no longer need to worry about regularly rebalancing these funds, either, but only the small portion they still have invested for growth. They have additional peace of mind as their worries about future market movements have also all but disappeared.

The sales of immediate annuities have surged recently, up 47 percent in the first quarter of 2014 over the same quarter of 2013, according to insurance industry research group LIMRA, and their sales are projected to steadily grow. However, this particular income product accounts for less than 10 percent of total annuity sales overall. Why? People simply don't understand how they work!

OTHER TYPES OF ANNUITIES AND GUARANTEED LIFETIME INCOME

There are other types of annuities that can also guarantee lifetime income aside from lifetime income annuities. Typically, these include variable annuities, deferred income annuities and fixed index annuities.

Variable Annuities

These are the annuities that everyone loves to hate due to their high fees. Although variable annuities typically have higher fees than a mutual fund, that doesn't make them bad from my point of view. If I could retire on low fees, the fees would matter. But I don't; I retire on where I can make the most and lose the least *after* fees. I want to make as much as I can without losing what I've already got!

With the variable annuity, I can invest in a family of sub-accounts, which is similar to mutual funds. I can have the upside of the stock, bond, and commodity markets; but because of the guarantees that a variable annuity offers, I can sleep at night whenever the market crashes knowing that my survivors will be protected should the unexpected occur.

This is because variable annuities typically have a death benefit guarantee: If the market crashes, your family will get back no less than what you invested. Many of these products also have a ratchet feature that will allow you to "lock in" market gains periodically, such as on each policy anniversary.

However, most attention has recently focused on the guaranteed living benefits. A guaranteed withdrawal benefit is the most common. With this, you are guaranteed a minimum amount that you can withdraw each year. Even if the account runs out of money, you are guaranteed this income for the rest of your life. Some will even give you joint life income, guaranteeing a minimum withdrawal benefit for the rest of your life and your spouse's.

Many times, variable annuities also have a "roll up" benefit, or guaranteed growth of a percentage (for example, 5 percent) of the benefit base. This base is normally the amount of money you put into the contract plus any previous increases due to the guaranteed roll up. However, this roll up amount is different than your cash value. Your cash value can (and will) go up and down based on market returns and any withdrawals. You must be very careful, because if you make any changes to your withdrawals, it can wipe out some of the guarantees.

After the guaranteed withdrawal benefit is the guaranteed income benefit, which also typically has a roll up–type of guarantee. The difference from a withdrawal benefit guarantee is that the income benefit is "locked in" – it is an annuitized benefit, so there is not much flexibility. I would argue that the withdrawal benefit has less flexibility than many people realize, but it is a little more flexible than the guaranteed income benefit.

The last type of guarantee is the least common, but it is the one that I personally own. It is the accumulation value guarantee, which is a cash value guarantee, not an income guarantee. The accumulation value guarantee allows you to capture much – or all – of the upside of the market but puts a "floor" under the cash value. Some guarantees will allow you to lock in market gains periodically. However, the guarantee is normally for a 10 to 15 year period of time, so you need to be willing to hold the annuity for 10 to 15 years if we experience a bear market.

Deferred Income Annuities

The second type of annuity may be the fastest growing – the deferred income annuity, which is very similar to the lifetime income annuity. Both offer guaranteed lifetime income; both pay longevity credits. The only real difference is in the timing of the income. A lifetime income annuity must start paying income within 13 months of purchase and normally starts the next month after the annuity is purchased. A deferred income annuity starts anywhere from 2 to 50 years or more after purchase.

For example, a 45-year-old male could purchase a deferred income annuity that would start paying income at age 65 with a 15 percent guaranteed payout rate. If the 45-year-old put in $100,000 today, he would be guaranteed about $15,000 per year for the rest of his life, starting at age 65.

While some of you may think that you could do better by investing in stocks or real estate, you are not *guaranteed*. While guarantees are subject to the claims-paying ability of the insurance company, it is important to note that *all* guaranteed lifetime income annuities have paid their guaranteed payouts to their purchasers.

While I don't advocate putting all of your money into any one product, I do advocate putting some of your money into guaranteed lifetime income products. These products guarantee income for not only the original annuitant, but could also provide guarantees for heirs.

Bob Hartman, a financial professional in Carefree, Arizona, had a client who had been relying on traditional tax-free fixed income investments for his retirement income. Once Bob described the features of the lifetime income annuity, the client decided to purchase a one-time fixed annuity. After some experience with his annuity, coupled with the declining income from his traditional fixed income investments, the client contacted Bob and placed additional funds into the plan.

The client then stipulated that his beneficiaries must purchase lifetime income annuities with their inheritance; he wanted to help his heirs without ruining their lives by giving them large blocks of money. During this time, deferred income annuities became very popular in the industry. So Bob wrote a deferred income annuity on each of the beneficiaries. Going forward, the client plans to add additional funds each year into each of the deferred income policies. Upon the client's death, what is left of his estate will also be divided into each of his heirs' deferred income annuities.

Once people "get" the concept of guaranteed lifetime income, it's easy to see why retirees who can rely on it are so much happier.

Fixed Index Annuities

The final type of annuity product is the fixed index annuity. With the fixed index annuity, the principal and the interest are guaranteed, the cash value does not go down if the market goes down (like a variable annuity), but the cash value also does not go up with the market.

The account will be credited with guaranteed interest based on a formula that takes a market index performance into account. Many of these products are capped on the upside but cannot pay below 0 percent. For example, if the S&P 500 was up 19 percent, the index annuity might credit 4 or 5 percent; if the market was down 19 percent, the index annuity might credit 0 percent.

For a number of years, I was not a fan of index annuities because they typically had long surrender periods and high surrender charges. But after I read *The Power of Zero*, I saw how *not losing* money in the down years was as important as, if not more important than, making money in the good years. In addition, the income benefits of index annuities are often as good as – and sometimes better than – the benefits of variable annuities.

While I personally don't own index annuities, I do believe that they can play a viable role in retirement planning. It is important to deal with a trusted financial professional in analyzing your options when making your plan.

WHICH ANNUITY IS BEST?

This is a question that can best be determined by you and your financial professional. However, I will give you some of my guidance.

First, the biggest determining factor is age. According to Dr. Moshe Milevsky, there is overwhelming evidence that people over the age of 70 should use a lifetime income annuity because the mortality or longevity credits are just too significant to ignore.

Before age 60, a variable, index, or deferred income annuity would probably be more appropriate. The variable annuity would give you the most possible upside potential; the deferred income annuity would give you the greatest guaranteed future income; and the index annuity would be somewhere in between. It depends on your particular situation and what you value most in an income-producing product.

Between the ages of 60 and 70, it depends on when you are planning to retire and how conservative you are. The more conservative you are, the more you should lean toward the lifetime income annuity or the deferred income annuity. The more aggressive you are, the more you should look into a variable or index annuity.

One other key feature that many people overlook is creditor protection, which varies by state. In Arizona, for example, all of the money that I have in life insurance and annuities is creditor protected. I would recommend speaking with your licensed financial advisor to determine the laws in your home state.

If you are a doctor, dentist, chiropractor, small business owner, etc., getting sued is one of the largest risks that you face. Money in mutual funds and brokerage accounts can be sued. Then what happens to your retirement plans?
It is important to realize here, though, that just because you have an annuity doesn't mean you can't be sued - it just means that in certain states and in certain cases, creditors *may* not be able to get

to those particular assets in a lawsuit. Creditors such as the IRS and state taxing authorities can most likely reach some or all of the funds - and absolute protection from creditors is not a given in all states. For more information on how different types of assets are and aren't creditor-protected, visit:

www.investopedia.com/articles/retirement/07/buildawall.asp

The bottom line is that income is what pays the mortgage, the utilities, and the grocery bill. Concentrating on net worth in retirement won't get you very far. In fact, Nobel laureate Robert C. Merton was recently quoted as saying, "The seeds of an investment crisis have been sown. The only way to avoid a catastrophe is for [retirement] plan participants, professionals, and regulators to shift the mindset and metrics from asset value to income." I couldn't agree more.

KEY CHAPTER POINTS

- Having enough guaranteed lifetime income can not only make or break the type of lifestyle you have in retirement but also the type of life you live.
- The happiest people are those who have sources of guaranteed lifetime income. Securing at least a base level of lifetime income should be every retiree's priority.
- The real goal of the retirement savings we accumulate is to convert those funds into a livable, ongoing income for our retirement.
- There is no "magic number." The accumulation phase of saving for retirement is only the end of the beginning; the distributions from your savings have absolutely, positively got to last until the end.
- Distributing assets in a way that ensures you get the most out of your retirement without running out of money is a difficult balancing act that should, quite frankly, be taken even more seriously than the accumulation phase of your retirement savings.

- When planning for your golden years, you need to think less about how much money you have saved and more about how you will spread out what you have so that it will last in terms of income for the rest of your life.
- There are several sources of guaranteed lifetime income. These include Social Security, pension benefits, and annuity payouts.
- Lifetime income annuities pay out based on mortality credits, which work as a type of "bonus"—the longer you live, the more bonus you receive.
- By allocating a portion of your portfolio to some of the more inflation-sensitive investments, you can optimize your portfolio in order to protect against inflation, while at the same time ensure that income needs are being met for life through the lifetime income annuity.
- According to retirement experts, the lifetime income annuity is the one retirement solution that can help every American secure a guaranteed lifetime income.
- Among retirees with similar wealth and health characteristics, those with incomes from annuities are happiest.
- Variable annuities, index annuities, and deferred income annuities all offer guaranteed income as well as other guarantees.
- Money invested in life insurance and annuities is creditor protected in some states. "The only way to avoid a catastrophe is for [retirement] plan participants, professionals, and regulators to shift the mindset and metrics from asset value to income," according to Nobel laureate Robert C. Merton.

Step 6:
You Must Have a Plan for Long-Term Care

Many people think that retirement is going to be 30 to 40 years of golf, tennis, cruises, and happy hours. But that is not true – you will likely go through three distinct phases in your retirement.

The first phase I call the "Go Go" years. These are those early years of retirement when you are golfing, playing tennis, traveling, and enjoying your retirement. Unfortunately, the Go Go years are followed by the "Slow Go" years. The Slow Go years are when you can still do everything that you did in the Go Go years, but you just don't want to. In fact, you don't want to go downtown after 4:30 pm because Dad can't see when it's dark out! The Slow Go years are followed by the "No Go" years, when you're probably not leaving the building, until you're "leaving the building."

When planning for your retirement, you need to keep all three phases of retirement in mind. They will remind you to fully enjoy your early years and to adjust your retirement expenses over time. That is why Step 6 will discuss why you absolutely must have a plan for long-term care.

Did you know that one of the fastest ways to exhaust your retirement savings is to be ambushed by the costs of long-term care? With Step 6, you will plan for long-term care and other medical costs so that you will not be surprised by unexpected medical bills during your retirement.

REAL SPENDING IN RETIREMENT

Retirement research has increasingly shown that retirees experience a decline in spending throughout their retirement, as the early Go Go years transition to the less active Slow Go years and then eventually into the No Go years. With this in mind, you may want to allocate more of your money toward travel and entertainment early in your retirement and more toward your medical expenses later on.

At age 65, if you are not covered by a corporate medical insurance plan, most Americans qualify for Medicare for their regular health insurance expenses. In 2013, more than 50 million people received healthcare benefits through Medicare. It is the largest public healthcare system in the United States, with 85 percent of beneficiaries over the age of 65. Anyone who pays into Social Security during their working years also pays into Medicare. If you haven't paid into the system, you have the option to buy Medicare at age 65.

Even though Medicare is the nation's largest healthcare system, its coverage does have holes. According to the US Department of Health and Human Services, Medicare pays only 55 percent of healthcare costs for its enrollees. The costs that aren't covered by Medicare must be paid by you – by your savings or through a supplemental insurance policy. In order to cover the shortfalls in their Medicare coverage, retirees will often use medical coverage from their former employers or they will purchase a Medicare supplement insurance plan once they turn 65. These plans typically pay the costs that Medicare doesn't pay, including the deductibles, copayments, and coinsurance. But they don't pay for long-term care.

FALLING INTO MEDICARE'S ADDITIONAL COVERAGE GAPS

There are still gaps in Medicare's coverage, and long-term care represents the largest of those gaps. Let me repeat: Medicare does *not* pay for most long-term care.

This gap can heavily impact your monthly retirement income. Within a short period of time, it could also wipe out your entire retirement savings if not properly planned for. You've likely heard stories about retirees who lost everything because they had to go into a nursing home for a lengthy period of time. It can happen. Long-term care is expensive, and, unfortunately, many people find out too late that most of these costs aren't covered by Medicare or their regular health insurance plan. In addition, many people simply don't believe (or don't want to believe) that they'll need long-term care.

According to AARP, about two-thirds of today's older Americans will require long-term care at some point in their lives.

One way to control these costs is to purchase long-term care insurance.

WHO REALLY "NEEDS" LONG-TERM CARE?

When I ask a room full of people who needs long-term care, most agree that a large percentage of people will eventually need some type of care as they get older. The problem is, nobody thinks that *they* will be the ones who will need it. According to LIMRA, "There is a disconnect between the concern retirees exhibit over health-related risks in retirement and the product development and advice provided by the financial services industry. Similarly, retirees are not covering some of these risks by enrolling in Medicare Part D or purchasing long-term care insurance."

Nine out of every ten Medicare beneficiaries suffer with one or more chronic illnesses, according to the Kaiser Foundation. Nearly half of the Medicare population who are age 65 and over have three or more chronic conditions. Among Medicare enrollees, nearly one in four individuals age 65 to 84 are limited in their ability to handle even some of the most basic activities of daily living, such as bathing and eating, with a similar share of these individuals being limited in their ability to do instrumental daily activities, such as housework and meal preparation.

The biggest challenge that retirees face in planning for healthcare expenses in retirement is uncertainty. This uncertainty comes from not knowing about their ultimate life expectancy, healthcare needs, or how much health and long-term care expense they will incur. From a financial standpoint, the best way to combat this is to include long-term care in your retirement planning.

No retirement plan is complete without a plan for long-term care. For many seniors, this is the only thing for which they have not planned that could completely eliminate their life savings within a very short period of time.

Let's put this into perspective. If your house burned to the ground, it would be an emotional loss, but your homeowner's insurance would cover you. Likewise, if you totaled your car, you may have some physical injuries, but the insurance company would protect you. What would happen if you needed full-time, around-the-clock care to help you live your life? What would that cost? How long would your savings last? What would happen to your spouse and family?

The odds of your home burning down between now and the day you die are only about 3 out of 100, or 3 percent, but nearly every homeowner has homeowner's insurance. The odds of totaling your car between now and the day you die are about 18 out of 100, or 18 percent, yet nearly every automobile owner carries automobile insurance. The odds that you will need some form of long-term care between now and the day you die are about 72 out of 100, or 72 percent. However, less than 30 percent of Americans over the age of 45 have purchased long-term care insurance to protect themselves from this need.

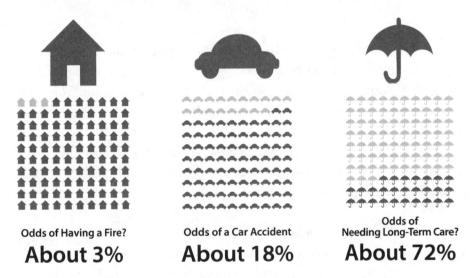

Odds of Having a Fire?
About 3%

Odds of a Car Accident
About 18%

Odds of Needing Long-Term Care?
About 72%

According to Genworth's 2014 Cost of Care Survey, the national median daily rate of a semi-private room in a skilled nursing facility is currently $212, or $77,380 per year. A private room bumps the price tag up to $240 per day, or just under $88,000 per year. Assisted care facilities are somewhat less, coming in at $3,500 per month, or $42,000 per year. Depending on the particular health condition and need, a person could be paying these costs for quite a while, too. According to the American Association for Long-Term Care Insurance, the average length of stays in a nursing home can vary considerably.

AVERAGE LENGTH OF STAYS IN A SKILLED NURSING HOME

5 years or more	12.0%
3 to 5 years	12.0%
1 to 3 years	30.3%
6 to 12 months	14.2%
3 to 6 months	11.5%
Less than 3 months	20.0%

Since most long-term care is actually received at home, it's important to have a good understanding of the cost of in-home care assistance as well because, depending on the situation, this may come out to be more costly in the long run. Today, according to Genworth, the national median hourly rate of a home health aide is $20, while that of homemaker services is $19, although the private pay rate for a Medicare-certified home health agency can be considerably higher.

Any of these costs would involve taking a considerable hit to most retirees' portfolios, especially for a healthy spouse who was relying on income and growth from the couple's portfolio for living expenses and combating inflation. Protecting you and your spouse from this potential threat to retirement assets is crucial.

In fact, my colleague Peter D'Arruda ("Coach Pete") sums it up best when he says that no one is any safer than the person who has looked ahead and shifted the financial burden from their family to an insurance company in the form of life or long-term care insurance. There's really no better way to bring peace of mind with you into retirement. He goes on to say that the secret to a happy retirement is to identify the potential shortfalls in your financial plan by finding what's truly needed for your specific situation.

Then, by honestly assessing what needs to be accomplished through the use of tools and strategies that are available today, you can eliminate potential problems in the future. The bottom line: Make sure that you never leave your family in a situation where they have to change zip codes upon your death!

THE MANY MYTHS ABOUT WHO PAYS FOR LONG-TERM CARE

Nationally, Medicare covers only about 5 percent of long-term care costs. In order to qualify for Medicare's skilled nursing facility coverage through Part A, you must meet fairly strict requirements, including the following:

- Your doctor must certify that you need daily skilled care as provided by, or under the direct supervision of, a skilled nursing or rehabilitation staff.
- You must have a minimum three-day hospital stay, not including the day of discharge, preceding your entry into the skilled nursing facility.
- Your entry into the skilled nursing facility must be for the same condition for which you were hospitalized.
- Your condition must be considered recuperative, meaning that if you have an ongoing condition such as Alzheimer's disease or Parkinson's disease from which you will not recuperate, you will not qualify.

Even if you do qualify, you may still need to pay a substantial amount of money out-of-pocket due to Medicare's considerable coverage gaps. Here's how it breaks down:

- "You pay nothing for the first 20 days."
- "You pay [a copayment of] $152 per day for days 21–100" (in 2014).
- "You pay all costs for each day after day 100."

Provided that you need a lengthy period of care following an accident with several months of rehabilitation, you'd be out $12,160 (the 80 days of co-pay).

Medicare covers a minute amount of home care under Part B; however, the services must be deemed medically necessary, a Medicare term that means "healthcare services or supplies needed to prevent, diagnose, or treat an illness, injury, condition, disease, or its symptoms and that meet accepted standards of medicine." Medicare requires that home care services be ordered by a doctor and that you are receiving skilled treatment for an illness or injury. Help with bathing, dressing, and toileting are not considered to be medically necessary; they are considered custodial care. In addition, Medicare will not pay for room and board at an assisted living facility or adult daycare. Only services that are considered medically necessary for the treatment of a specific medical condition are covered.

What about the other government program, Medicaid? The good news is that Medicaid was developed in large part for covering the costs of long-term care, primarily for those who are in nursing home facilities. The bad news is that Medicaid is essentially for people who are destitute. It is actually a form of welfare; in addition to having a medical need, it requires a means test in order to qualify.

To be eligible for Medicaid's long-term care coverage, you will need to spend down nearly all of your savings before Medicaid will kick in. Because Medicaid is actually a joint federal-state program, the qualification requirements can differ from one state to another. Although there are hundreds of different sets of eligibility rules for Medicaid's long-term care services, here is a partial list from 2014 of the financial resources that may be at risk:

- Assets of between $2,000 and $15,000 (depending on your state)
- Primary home equity (the amount also depends on your state)
- Most personal income, although there are some rules in place to prevent total impoverishment of a healthy spouse
- Retirement accounts (eg, 401(k), IRA)
- Cash value life insurance
- Vacation home, second vehicles

In the past, many people thought that they could simply shift assets to family members in order to get them out of their own name. This, however, isn't the way it works. When you initially apply for benefits, Medicaid will take a five-year look back of your financial statements. They do this in order to search for any asset transfers that you may have given to your family or to others. If it is discovered that you either transferred or sold a personal asset, then that asset is considered "available" for your nursing home care and will disqualify you from Medicaid for a certain period of time.

Because you did not use that particular asset to pay for your care, the government will take the value of that asset and divide it by the average cost per day of a local nursing home. This will determine the length of your "penalty period," or the period of time that you will have to pay for all of your care expenses out-of-pocket before Medicaid will take over paying.

Presume that you gave $25,000 each to your two grandchildren in order to help them with a down payment on their houses. You made this gift three years before you applied for Medicaid. Suppose that the daily cost of a nursing home in your area is $150. Because you made the gift to your grandchildren less than five years prior to applying for benefits, Medicaid would take the total amount of the $50,000 you transferred out of your name and divide it by the $150 daily cost of nursing home care in your area. This gives you a total of roughly 333 days of care that you would need to pay for yourself out-of-pocket before you would qualify for Medicaid benefits. Where is the money for those 333 days of care going to come from? You've already given away $50,000 and that money has already been spent by the grandchildren on their new homes.

If you have income from Social Security, pension, or retirement investments, Medicaid will only cover the difference in the cost for your care. So, if your income is $3,000 per month and your care costs $5,000, Medicaid will only cover the $2,000 per month difference. Thanks to a process known as "estate recovery," Medicaid is also allowed to recoup any money that it spent on your care from your estate after you've passed away. Where will *that* money come from?

WHY PURCHASE A LONG-TERM CARE INSURANCE POLICY?

A long-term care insurance policy offers many benefits, including:

- **ASSET PROTECTION** – An unanticipated long-term care event can wipe out an individual's or a couple's entire life savings. Long-term care insurance shifts the cost of care to the insurance company and away from savings, which protects funds for their original intent.

- **PROTECTION OF A HEALTHY SPOUSE OR PARTNER** – It is important for couples to determine how one spouse's illness could affect the other financially. For those without long-term care insurance coverage, a spouse or partner may be forced to pay for a caregiver out of their joint savings and then be left with little to nothing for their own financial needs.

- **REMOVAL OF CAREGIVING BURDEN FROM LOVED ONES**
  – Oftentimes, the role of the care provider falls to family and
  other loved ones. While this may be with noble intent, it is also
  very costly. From a financial standpoint, the family must pay for
  such things as grab bars, canes and walkers, and gas for going to
  doctors' appointments. Emotionally, the role reversal of children
  caring for parents can be especially difficult. The toll physically of
  lifting, bathing, and caring for a family member continuously for
  an extended period of time can lead to hernias, back problems,
  and other serious issues. Long-term care insurance allows loved
  ones to pay for the proper type of care that is needed, while at the
  same time spending more quality time with the care recipient.

- **PEACE OF MIND** – If you are single or do not have any close
  relatives nearby, long-term care insurance can reassure you that
  your needs are going to be taken care of. This type of coverage
  can coordinate and pay for the care that you may need.

- **MAINTENANCE OF CONTROL, INDEPENDENCE,
  AND DIGNITY** – As opposed to those who lose control of their
  care choices when they go on Medicaid, those who have a long-
  term care insurance policy can retain much more say in how
  and where they receive the care that they need.

TODAY'S CARE CHOICES

Today, the variety of care choices has opened up – nursing homes
are not the only choice anymore – and long-term care insurance will
typically pay for many of these.

In most instances, people prefer to remain in their own home.
A home health aide would help you prepare meals, bathe and get
dressed, or perform some of the other routine activities of daily living.

If you enjoy the company of others but want the freedom to come and go as you please, you may decide to join the 750,000 Americans who live in assisted living facilities across the country.

There are also thousands of continuing care retirement communities. You can move in while you are still in good health, and later, should your health deteriorate, you can transition to a higher level of personal care that better meets your needs.

LESSENING YOUR RISK WITH LONG-TERM CARE INSURANCE

With Medicare paying so little and Medicaid requiring you to spend down your assets, you only have two options to pay for the costs of long-term care. One is to use money from your savings; the other is to purchase a long-term care insurance policy.

Just like homeowner's and auto insurance, in return for a regular premium payment, long-term care insurance can protect you from what could be a devastating financial loss if you should need expensive care.

These types of policies typically pay for a spectrum of services, such as:

- Home care
- Assisted living facility or residential care facility
- Skilled nursing facility
- Hospice care
- Adult daycare

Many policies may also allocate funds for installing wheelchair ramps, grab bars, and other items that make it easier for you to remain in your home while receiving care.

In addition, long-term care insurance does not require a previous hospital stay before you can qualify for benefits, nor are you required to spend down your assets. You must simply meet the benefit triggers that are identified in the policy.

Long-term care insurance policies are constructed and priced based on several criteria. In most cases, you can choose the various options that you want on the policy to best fit with your specific needs. These factors include:

- Amount of benefit
- Length of time you want benefits to be paid (i.e., a certain number of years or a lifetime benefit option)
- Elimination period, which is the number of days that must pass before the policy benefits will begin to pay
- Inflation protection, which will increase your benefit amount over time in order to keep pace with the rising cost of care

Many of today's long-term care insurance policies may include riders that can be added in order to enhance coverage. For example, the Premium Refund Rider guarantees that your family will be refunded all of your premiums at your death if you never used the coverage. In addition, policies will typically provide premium discounts for couples if both apply for coverage at the same time.

In terms of paying for long-term care insurance, there are numerous options. Premium payments could be made out-of-pocket; however, many retirees opt to use the income from a lifetime income annuity to pay their long-term care insurance premium.

TYPES OF LONG-TERM CARE COVERAGE

Many of the long-term care insurance policies available in the marketplace today are stand-alone plans. This means that the policy is applied for and underwritten for an individual applicant, and the benefits are provided to that individual if and when they are triggered by a long-term care need.

However, there are other options available. Several insurance carriers now offer shared care. This type of policy is purchased by couples and funded by one single pool of benefits that can be accessed by either person. Typically, the premiums on these shared care policies are cheaper than purchasing two individual stand-alone plans.

There are also several types of combination long-term care plans on the market today. These "hybrid" or "linked products" can attach a long-term care rider to either a life insurance policy or an annuity. One benefit is that the purchaser knows that, one way or the other, they will gain some type of benefit from their premium payment even if they don't use it for a long-term care need.

For example, I recently saw an annuity for which, if a client purchased $3,000 a month of lifetime income, the amount doubled to $6,000 per month if they needed long-term care. However, there was a waiting period when no benefits could be claimed for the first three years. This type of annuity could be ideal for someone who knows they will need care sometime in the future but can't qualify for a regular long-term care insurance policy.

Another alternative is the combination life insurance and long-term care option. There are a couple of ways in which this type of plan can be set up. One option is a single premium life insurance policy set up as universal, whole, or variable universal life that allows the policyholder to deposit one lump sum and then receive a certain amount of long-term care benefit if needed. A named beneficiary would receive a death benefit from the policy if long-term care benefits are not needed. The long-term care benefit is typically a percentage of the lump sum in the life insurance policy. For example, if there is $200,000 in the policy and the long-term care benefit is 2 percent, then the policyholder would receive $4,000 per month for their long-term care benefit.

The other option for a life and long-term care policy is the optional rider plan. The policyholder purchases a life insurance policy with a long-term care benefit provided through an optional rider on the policy. Often, these plans will require a recurring premium payment. With this policy, the long-term care insurance rider allows the life insurance contract to be accessed for living benefits by paying down the face amount of the policy's death benefit. Any portion of the death benefit not paid out as long-term care coverage will be paid to a beneficiary when the insured passes away.

Regardless of how you cover the cost of your long-term care, it is essential to protect your retirement portfolio. Otherwise, a lifetime of savings could be gone within a short period of time.

IMPORTANT CONSIDERATIONS WHEN PURCHASING LONG-TERM CARE INSURANCE

Long-term care is the one big risk that can wipe out your entire life's work, but many people don't have insurance against this risk.

It is important to first keep in mind that you must qualify to purchase a long-term care insurance policy. Do not wait until you have a serious medical condition to apply because you most likely will not qualify. The younger you are when you apply, the lower the premiums will be. So, the sooner you apply, the better.

Look for a policy that is federally qualified. That way, the benefits you receive will be income tax free. This can make a big difference, especially if you needed thousands of dollars in benefits per month for several years.

The insurance company through which you purchase your policy should have high financial ratings and a history of integrity. Because you may not need your benefits for 20 years or more, you must be sure that the underlying insurance company exists in the future when you need it.

You should also seek out a comprehensive policy that offers a wide range of benefits. Everyone's needs are different at the time of a claim. Make sure that you include home health care coverage and inflation-adjusted benefit payments.

Be sure to select an elimination period that you can afford. Even though a longer elimination period will keep your premiums lower, you don't want the cost of the elimination period to be prohibitive.

If you are a federal employee, you should consider the Federal Long-Term Care Insurance Program. This plan provides long-term care insurance plans for federal employees, military members and their families.

Every day, there are new long-term care protection options being developed. Even if you aren't able to cover all of your potential risk, you must consider a plan to protect yourself from whatever you can. Your financial professional can help you to research your options.

When it comes to protection from the high cost of long-term care, ANY plan is better than NO plan at all.

KEY CHAPTER POINTS

- You will go through three distinct phases in your retirement.
- Retirees experience a decline in real spending through their retirement.
- Medicare does NOT pay for long-term care. This gap in Medicare's coverage can heavily impact your monthly retirement income. Within a fairly short period of time, it could wipe out your entire retirement savings if not properly planned for.
- No retirement plan is complete without a plan for long-term care.
- The odds that you will need some form of long-term care between now and the day you die are about 72 out of 100, or 72 percent!
- Medicaid is essentially for people who are destitute. It is actually a form of welfare.
- The only other choices for payment of long-term care are using money from your savings or purchasing a long-term care insurance policy.
- Long-term care is the one big risk that can wipe out your entire life's work, but many people don't have insurance to protect themselves from this risk.
- You must qualify for long-term care insurance, so do not wait until you have a serious medical condition before you apply.
- When it comes to protection from the high cost of long-term care, ANY plan is better than NO plan.

Step 7:
Use Home Equity Wisely

If you haven't put away a lot of money for retirement and if you own your home, this equity could be a viable source of additional retirement income. By home equity, I mean the worth of your home above the remaining balance on your mortgage. If you fall into this category, you may discover that your home is a very valuable retirement asset.

After all, for years it's been said that our home is the biggest investment we will ever make. In many instances, this could be true. Despite the recent mortgage crisis, many Americans still have a substantial amount of equity in their homes. A report by the National Reverse Mortgage Lenders Association found that Americans age 62 and older hold approximately $4.3 trillion in home equity.

UNLOCKING THE EQUITY FROM YOUR HOME

In the past, many retirees automatically sold the family home and downsized; today, there are a growing number of seniors who, for one reason or another, are hanging onto their homes and taking advantage of the equity.

There are several ways that retirees can access the equity in their homes. The most commonly used ways include:

- Selling the house and downsizing
- Taking a loan against the home equity
- Getting a reverse mortgage

The first two ways are generally well-understood. The third, getting a reverse mortgage, requires some explanation.

According to a recent CNN Money report, "Reverse mortgages, that were once considered options of last resort, are now poised to become a mainstream financial strategy for older adults looking to shore up their retirements."

The reverse mortgage uses this equity without having to move out of the house or to even make repayments until a time in the future. For many retirees, this can prove to be a win-win situation.

EXPLORING THE REVERSE MORTGAGE

Reverse mortgages are still a relatively new concept in the financial services world, especially as a source of retirement income for seniors. These financial vehicles allow their borrowers to tap into the equity of their home in order to use the money to pay for living expenses or for any other manner they see fit.

Reverse mortgages are also referred to as conversion mortgages. The borrower is not required to make any payments, nor do they need an income to qualify. Likewise, the borrower's credit is not an issue when determining whether or not an individual or couple will qualify, since the loan's collateral is the equity that is in the borrower's own home.

There are differing opinions about the wisdom of a reverse mortgage, and this option may not be right for you. To some experts, reverse mortgages are controversial. But, for many people, these financial vehicles work out quite well.

There are typically several ways in which you can receive your money through a reverse mortgage. These include:

- **LINE OF CREDIT** – Similar to a home equity line of credit, you can tap into a pool of money at various times whenever money is needed.

- **REGULAR PAYMENTS** – A regular payment schedule can be set up, such as monthly, for a certain period of time.

- **MODIFIED TERM** – This option is a combination of the monthly payments with the line of credit for a set period of time that is chosen up front by the borrower.

You can get a good idea of how much you'll receive through a reverse mortgage based on the amount of your home's equity and other pertinent factors by using one of the many reverse mortgage calculators found online.

The key criteria in determining how much can be borrowed include:

- Your zip code
- Your birth date
- Your spouse's birth date, if applicable
- (if there is more than one borrower on the home, the age of the youngest borrower will be used in determining the amount that you can borrow)
- The value of your home
- The amount of any mortgages and other liens on your home
- The amount of the monthly payments on your mortgages

Additional information that a lender may ask for includes:

- The amount of other upfront cash that you desire
- An estimate of any necessary home repairs
- Your desired line-of-credit amount

WILL YOU QUALIFY FOR A REVERSE MORTGAGE?

There are several requirements that must be met in order to qualify for a reverse mortgage.

The Federal Housing Administration (FHA) requires that the homeowner be at least 62 years old. You must either own the home outright or have a very low mortgage balance; in other words, you must have a fairly large amount of equity in the home. If you do have a remaining mortgage balance, you are required to pay it off when you close on the reverse mortgage. You must also live in the home. The property can be a single family home, a HUD-qualified condo or manufactured home, or a one- to four-unit home where you live in one of the four units.

Prior to applying for a reverse mortgage, you will be required to obtain additional information from an approved home equity conversion mortgage counselor.

Similar to other types of loans, there are certain costs associated with obtaining a reverse mortgage. These typically include:

- "Loan origination fee"
- "Third-party fees (i.e., appraisal, inspection, lender title policy, etc.)"
- "FHA mortgage insurance premiums"
- "[Loan] servicing fee"
- "Interest"

IS A REVERSE MORTGAGE RIGHT FOR YOU?

There are benefits to having a reverse mortgage for supplementing your retirement income as long as you understand the potential downfalls.

Why has a reverse mortgage been a miracle for some people but a nightmare for others? For some, their home equity is the only equity they have and receiving income from that equity has allowed them to live a much better lifestyle in retirement. Others, though, have had problems when they tried to move to a different home.

If you go with a reverse mortgage, you will still be responsible for all of the costs associated with home ownership, such as insurance and property taxes as well as the home's maintenance. If you are unable to keep up with those payments, you could lose the house.

A reverse mortgage may, however, make sense if you've built up a good amount of equity in your home, if you plan to stay there as your primary residence, and if you won't have enough income to meet your living expenses in retirement with your Social Security and other income sources.

My advice is to be careful if you're considering a reverse mortgage. Do your homework and work with a trusted financial professional.

CONSIDERATIONS BEFORE MOVING FORWARD WITH A REVERSE MORTGAGE

The only reverse mortgage insured by the United States federal government is a Home Equity Conversion Mortgage (HECM), and this type of reverse mortgage is only available through an FHA-approved lender. Be sure that you're dealing with a reputable and legitimate reverse mortgage lender if you're going this route.

You cannot be forced by a lender to sell your home for the purpose of repaying the loan. You are allowed to remain in your home for as long as you like, even if the outstanding loan balance, plus interest, is more than the value of the property. If a lender is indicating anything to the contrary, you will want to seek a different lender. (Remember to always read all of the fine print prior to signing on the dotted line.)

The loan generally does not have to be repaid until the last surviving homeowner either passes away or has permanently moved out of the property. Even if your spouse has passed away, you have a right to remain in the home if you would like to do so.

When the home is sold or it is no longer being used as a primary residence, the cash, interest, and other finance charges that are related to the reverse mortgage must then be repaid to the lender. All of the proceeds beyond the amount that are owed will belong to your estate, meaning that any remaining equity can then be transferred to your heirs. Therefore, no debt is passed along to your beneficiaries.

BRINGING HOME AN EXAMPLE

Bill and Briana had purchased a $300,000 home many years ago that they have since paid off. After doing some investigating, they discover that they can use some of their home equity to supplement their retirement income through a reverse mortgage. However, they decide to use equity in a different way. Their residence had accumulated $150,000 in capital gains, so they opted to move into a smaller home, which they purchased for $150,000.

They sold their current home and took a tax-free capital gains exclusion. This move enabled them to add all $150,000 tax free to their retirement savings. That's what I call using your home equity wisely!

KEY CHAPTER POINTS

- Your home equity could be a viable source of additional retirement income for you.
- Reverse mortgage borrowers are not required to make any payments, nor do they need an income in order to qualify.
- You must be at least 62 years old to qualify for a reverse mortgage, and you must own your home as well as reside in it.
- There are several costs associated with obtaining a reverse mortgage.
- For some retirees, a reverse mortgage has been a miracle, but, for others, these financial vehicles have been a nightmare; it is important to be sure that this is a good solution for you and your specific needs by weighing all of your options prior to moving forward with one.
- A reverse mortgage may make sense if you've built up a good amount of equity in your home, if you plan to stay in the home for at least several more years as your primary residence, and if you won't have enough income to meet your living expenses in retirement with your Social Security and other income sources.
- You cannot be forced by a lender to sell your home for the purpose of repaying the reverse mortgage loan. You are allowed to remain in your home for as long as you like, even if the outstanding loan balance, plus interest, is more than the value of the property.
- A reverse mortgage loan generally does not have to be repaid until the last surviving homeowner either passes away or has permanently moved out of the property.
- When the home is sold or it is no longer being used as a primary residence, the cash, interest, and other finance charges related to the reverse mortgage must then be repaid. All of the proceeds beyond the amount that are owed will belong to the estate, meaning that any remaining equity can then be transferred to your heirs. No debt is passed along to your beneficiaries.

Some Extra Tips for Those Who Have Started Late

Those who have put off saving for retirement for any reason may feel that it's too late and that there's no hope. But it's never too late. By creating a plan, setting realistic financial goals, and understanding income-increasing strategies, you will be able to contribute significantly to your nest egg and boost the amount of income that you receive from other sources, such as Social Security.

It may take a bit more effort and strategizing, but you will get there. It will be imperative to stay focused and stick with your plan because, as the old saying goes, "time is money."

GETTING YOUR FINANCIAL DUCKS IN A ROW – EVEN WITH A LATE START

As you approach retirement, you must get your savings in order. After all, this aspect of your life is going to dictate how you will be able to live throughout the remainder of your retirement years.

Reset Your Money Mindset

The first thing that you will need to do is reset your money mindset: Be focused on the end result, regardless of the distractions and tough times that lie ahead. The best way to stay focused on your goal is to have a plan. A plan will keep you from becoming overwhelmed by the irrelevant financial information and will help you to attain – and maintain – your momentum going forward.

Pay Yourself First

As I mentioned in Step 4, pay yourself first. It bears repeating, especially if you've had a late start. Let's take an extreme example: You and your spouse, both age 50, are on a tight budget and you can each set aside only $10 per day in savings. You both plan to retire at age 70. Here's what it would look like:

YOU: $10 PER DAY X 365 DAYS = $3,650 PER YEAR
YOUR SPOUSE: $10 PER DAY X 365 DAYS = $3,650 PER YEAR
TOTAL: $7,300 PER YEAR

If you and your spouse were able to save $7,300 per year for 20 years, it could have a great impact on your future. At a 10% compounded rate, it would approach $500,000. Even at a 5% compounded rate, it would be hundreds of thousands of dollars.

De-clutter the House and Add to Your Account

One way to give your bank account a boost while cleaning out the attic, garage, or basement is to sell unwanted or unneeded items. There are numerous ways to do this, starting with popular online sites like eBay and Craigslist. Depending on the items you've collected, you could earn a substantial amount within a relatively short period of time.

In de-cluttering, you may also be helping yourself in other ways. For example, if you plan to eventually downsize, this could be a good start on clearing out items you won't want to take with you.

Cut Your Spending!

If you look back over your life, why have you not saved more money—because you haven't earned enough or because you spent more than you should have? For most people, it's the latter.

I have seen people who never made over $30,000 per year retire comfortably, while couples who made hundreds of thousands of dollars approach retirement almost penniless. Too many new cars, boats, jet skis, fancy vacations, etc. If this sounds familiar, it is time to become more frugal. Frugal doesn't mean that you can't have fun anymore. It simply means staying at the Comfort Inn instead of the Ritz Carlton and buying the used car, not the brand new one.

If you can save 10 percent, 15 percent, or even 50 percent on a purchase, it is the same as earning that money in the stock market. There are even websites dedicated to showing you how easy it is to live on a modest budget.

Work for a Few More Years

By working for a few more years, you can add significantly to your retirement income. You would be able to continue contributing to your savings, including your employer-sponsored retirement plan with employer-matching contributions, if offered. In addition, receiving income from your employer delays digging into your portfolio for retirement income. Each dollar that you earn while working is a dollar that doesn't need to be taken out of your retirement savings. In turn, this reduces the number of years that your savings will need to generate income for you, which is beneficial given our longer life expectancy. You could also stay on your group health insurance coverage, which can be a real plus, especially if you aren't yet age 65 and eligible for Medicare health insurance benefits.

By waiting to take your Social Security retirement benefits, you can rack up delayed retirement credits. For anyone born in 1943 or later, for each year that you delay taking benefits after your full retirement age, up to age 70, you can increase your retirement income by 8 percent per year.

A recent study found that a person who works for just an additional three years beyond age 62, saves 25 percent of their gross income, and delays collecting their Social Security benefits would increase their retirement income by 28 percent.

Earn More on the Side

In addition to working a few more years at your regular job, you should consider getting part-time work. You can add even more incoming cash flow and, if you're already living comfortably on what you earn from your full-time job, you can save 100 percent of the part-time job's wages.

Today, there are many opportunities available for part-time work with flexible hours. Many companies even allow you to "telecommute," meaning that you perform the work from home. Likewise, the Internet has created work-at-home opportunities on your own schedule. Just be careful that the job is legitimate. If it requires you to pay a large fee up front just to get started, this is usually a sign of a scam.

Open a Roth IRA

You should consider opening and funding a Roth IRA account if you haven't already done so. Provided that your annual income is under the maximum thresholds, you can contribute to a Roth IRA in addition to an employer-sponsored retirement plan, such as a 401(k). Although the contributions won't be tax deductible, the growth within the Roth account, as well as the withdrawals, will be tax free.

The maximum annual contribution limit for a Roth IRA in 2014 is $5,500 if you are under age 49; if you are over age 50, you are

SUMMARY	FULLY-TAXABLE	TAX-DEFERRED	TAX-FREE
Current investment balance	$0	$0	$0
Annual contributions	$6,500	$6,500	$6,500
Number of years to invest	20	20	20
Before-tax return	5%	5%	5%
Marginal tax return	28%	28%	28%
After-tax return	3.6%	5%	5%
Future account value*	$185,718	$214,929	$214,929
Future account value (after-tax)	$185,718	$191,149	$214,929

allowed an additional $1,000 "catch up" contribution for a total of $6,500. Even if you started a Roth IRA at age 50 and made a contribution of $6,500 per year over the next 20 years, with a 5 percent return you would have a nice additional amount to add to your retirement nest egg in comparison to a fully taxable account or even to a tax-deferred account.

*The lump sum shown after taxes is based on the 28 percent marginal tax rate. This lump sum after-tax figure does not take into account the possible change in tax bracket that might occur due to a lump sum distribution of the taxable amount, nor does it take into effect any applicable tax penalties.

Get Out of Debt

Although there are options to help get your retirement savings up to speed, they may not do you much good if you are in debt and paying out high amounts of interest every month to credit card companies or other lenders. In many ways, you'll probably be earning a negative return on what you're gaining from your investments if the loan interest rate is high.

If you are carrying large credit card balances or other types of debt with high rates of interest, start paying as much as possible toward these debts until they are fully paid off. You would be surprised at how much it can free up to put toward your retirement savings.

Consider Downsizing

Downsizing to a smaller or less costly living arrangement may make sense for your situation. If your kids have left the nest and you're paying to heat and cool areas of your home that are no longer being used, what you can save in utilities, mortgage, and property tax payments from downsizing can be shifted over and added to your retirement savings.

If you choose to downsize, consider relocating and moving to another area of the country altogether. By going somewhere with a lower cost of living, you can add what you save in living expenses to your retirement nest egg.

Take That Job!

For whatever reason – economic issues, problems with a particular business, etc. – you may become downsized or lose your job.

This can be a particularly tough blow if you were earning an income in the six figures; it is easy to see why you may not want to settle for a new job earning anything less. All too often, I see individuals in their late fifties or early sixties looking for a job opportunity that they may never find. In seeking this "needle in a haystack," they begin to burn through their savings and investments just to pay the bills until they find that comparable job.

My advice is not to hold out for a job with the same income level that you were earning before. Take a job with lesser pay if one is offered to you in order to get your incoming cash flowing again as soon as possible. If you've gotten a late start with your retirement savings, this is especially important, as you could end up using all of the money that you *have* saved during your search for the ideal job.

Get Started Now!

Regardless of how good the strategies are that you've learned from this book, if you don't get started NOW, you may never do it. Starting late is one thing, but the best financial advice in the world can't help the person who doesn't *ever* get started.

Tying It All Together

The strategies we've discussed in this book can solidly help you to secure your retirement, just like they helped my friend Betty. Betty was smart and took advantage of many of the retirement solutions that I've shared.

At 57, Betty was a teacher at a private school that didn't offer a pension plan. She was making contributions into an IRA regularly, but she didn't have enough to retire when she and her husband divorced after 28 years of marriage. Because her grandmother lived until she was 104, Betty was concerned about outliving her money and maintaining her current standard of living throughout her entire retirement.

Betty met with a financial professional, and together they prepared her retirement plan. In order to reach her goal, Betty took a new position at a public school that offered a pension plan. She sold her home to move into a house with other teachers in order to reduce her living expenses, and she put a portion of her equity into mutual funds. She also started deducting money every payday to put in her mutual funds. She had originally hoped to retire at age 65 but had to postpone her decision because her stock investments took a nosedive right before the date she had targeted.

She opted for a hybrid retirement strategy. She continued to work, reduce her expenses, and increase her savings. When Betty eventually retired, she began collecting a maximized Social Security benefit and moved some of her mutual fund and 401(k) money into a lifetime income annuity, using a portion of her retirement income to cover annual vacations with her girlfriends.

Instead of feeling concerned, Betty felt confident in the years leading up to her retirement. When she did retire, she had more guaranteed monthly income than she ever did while she was working!

Did you notice how Betty utilized many of my retirement security steps?

- She developed a retirement plan.
- She worked a little longer and saved a little more.
- She maximized her Social Security and secured some guaranteed lifetime income.
- She used her home equity wisely.
- She protected her savings from inflation.

In addition, Betty also has a plan for long-term care, should she need it in the future. Let's remember that Betty was already

57 years old when she started, newly divorced, with not enough money saved. If Betty can do it, you can too!

SOME TIPS FOR THOSE WHO *HAVE* SAVED FOR RETIREMENT

If you're in your fifties or sixties and you do have a respectable nest egg saved up, I have a few tips worth keeping in mind. As you may recall, the most important years for your portfolio are those immediately before and immediately after you retire.

For many who are approaching retirement, it is likely that you're earning more money now than in the past and spending less – the kids are out of college and the other big expenses have been paid off. With this in mind, you may be tempted to spend more than usual, especially if you've denied yourself in the past. I can't stress it enough to stay on course, avoid those expensive vacations or pricey shopping sprees, and continue socking money away for retirement. This is your chance to give your savings the extra boost it may need to increase your retirement income for the future. This could mean the difference between having enough over the long term and eventually running out.

Worse yet may be those times when you are tempted to dip into your savings in order to fund that "once in a lifetime" cruise or that vacation home that you may "never have the chance to buy again." Don't do it! Or, if you must treat yourself, try to do it "on sale." Many trips offer discounts for last-minute travel. I want you to enjoy your retirement; I want you to take cruises and to see the world—just do it wisely. Don't put your entire retirement in jeopardy for one trip. It's not worth risking future income for immediate gratification now, especially if what you're buying now isn't a necessity. Once you reach retirement, it's too late to change your mind and replace those lost savings. At that point, your only other option is to reduce your retirement lifestyle going forward.

Any situation that could set you back financially during those years just prior to retirement should be avoided at all costs. You don't have the time to start over. Even one wrong move can have an effect on the amount of income that you earn for the remainder of your retirement.

I would encourage you to do what I have done – buy future income! With deferred income annuities, you can safely lock in future guaranteed lifetime income at attractive payout rates. If you use a laddering strategy like I have done – guaranteed income that will start at age 60, more at 65 and 70, and even more at age 75 – you can guarantee that you will have increasing lifetime income for the rest of your life! If you are worried about the stock and commodity markets, this may be just the ticket for you.

KEY CHAPTER POINTS

- It is never too late to start saving for retirement.
- Cutting spending can be as important, if not more important, than increasing savings.
- It is imperative to stick with a plan and to stay focused because time is of the essence in order to succeed.
- This aspect of your life is going to dictate how you will be able to live throughout your retirement years.
- By saving just $10 per day, you could amass a large nest egg by the time you retire.
- Delaying Social Security income can increase benefits by 8 percent per year.
- Getting out of debt is essential to moving forward with retirement savings. Otherwise, you are just moving backward.
- Do not spend money that you have already saved, regardless of how tempting it may be to do so.
- Buy future lifetime income!

A Special Note to Women

While we all face risk with our retirement income, overall, women are subject to more financial risks than men, especially in their later years. Women have several disadvantages when it comes to retirement income, including an average longer lifespan then men, and many of these challenges can start early in their adult lives.

There are ways for women to overcome these financial challenges and achieve the optimal amount of income for their retirement years, provided that they are aware of what these challenges are and learn how to work around them.

GETTING HER FIRST JOB AT AGE 66

In "Lifetime Income for Women: A Financial Economist's Perspective" from July 2008, Dr. David Babbel tells a story about a couple he met. The husband had been educated at a top American university and had enjoyed a very successful career. Shortly before the husband had retired, his company changed from a defined-benefit pension plan to a defined-contribution retirement plan. When the husband retired, he took a generous lump sum settlement from the plan. His nephew convinced him to invest almost all of it into a "promising new opportunity" that the nephew would personally manage.

As you can expect, things went south quickly and they more or less lost their entire retirement savings. They had to remortgage the house. To make things worse, the husband's health began to fail. The wife, at age 66, had to get her first job to make ends meet. She now hopes to be able to retire at age 81 – not quite the retirement of their dreams.

This story brings to light an important point about retirement investing: Most people think that the older you are, the riskier the market is. This is not true. In reality, the riskiest time to invest your money is the five or six years before retirement and the five or six years after retirement. Losing money within this window can devastate your retirement, just as it did with this couple.

THE KEY RETIREMENT RISKS FACED BY WOMEN

In his report "Lifetime Income for Women: A Financial Economist's Perspective," Dr. David Babbel writes that American women, in particular, face five significant hurdles that impact their retirement income:

- "Decreasing rates of return on their Social Security contributions (averaging only 1.8 percent per year for single women)"

- "The accelerating demise of defined-benefit pension plans (150,000 pension plans, which would have provided lifetime income security, have been discontinued since 1983, leaving less than 25,000 plans today, many of which plan to close within two years)"

- "The transition of the baby boom generation into retirement (the first boomers reached retirement eligibility in 2006 and will continue to enter the retirement ranks over the next 20 years, creating a huge cash drain on our Social Security system)"

- "Longer expected lifetimes (65-year-old women have added another four years to their life expectancy since the 1960s; over the past 160 years, women in the most developed countries have steadily added another year to their life expectancy for each four years that pass)"

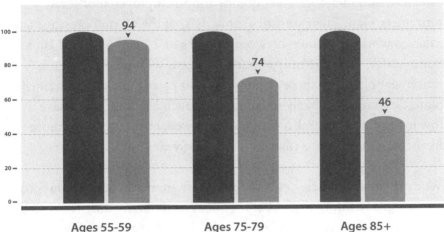

NUMBER OF MEN ALIVE PER 100 WOMEN AT VARIOUS AGES

● Women

- Roughly 75 percent of the nursing home residents are women, and women generally have much longer stays than men do in nursing homes, both likely stemming from their longer life expectancy. Because women are, for the most part, younger than their husbands, the wife will typically provide home care for her husband in his declining years, delaying the time before the husband needs to be cared for in a facility. However, less than 10 percent of females have a companion by the time their own health declines, so they need to seek institutional care. By that time, many couples' financial reserves have already been expended on the husband's care, leaving little money for the woman to spend on her own care.

- "The much smaller post–baby boom generations who are being asked to support boomers' unfunded benefits along with their own healthcare and retirement needs (and, owing to their greater life expectancy, women's benefits will be much costlier to fund than men's, all other things equal)"

In addition to these points from Babbel, the U.S. Department of Labor has found that women are more likely to work in part-time jobs and therefore don't qualify for an employer-sponsored retirement plan. Their statistics show that, of the 62 million wage and salaried working women between the ages of 21 and 64 in the United States today, there are only about 45 percent who participate in a retirement plan. For those women who do participate in a retirement plan, they are more likely to contribute much less and, thus, have a lower amount of overall savings, due to the fact that they are more likely than men to interrupt their working years to raise children.

Women are also much less risk tolerant than men when it comes to investing, according to Babbel's report. While many may think that this is a good thing—especially for those who are in retirement—by not having any of your money in equities or other inflation-fighting vehicles, your portfolio will be unable to keep up with the rising cost of goods and services.

SPECIFIC FINANCIAL CHALLENGES FACED BY TODAY'S WOMEN

While many women fall into more than one of the categories below, each will face certain specific challenges in ensuring they have enough income in retirement, especially given their longer life expectancy, which magnifies all of the other financial risks in retirement.

Single Women

There are more than 25 million single women in the United States over age 45, and that number is growing. There are many reasons for the tremendous growth in this segment of the population: divorce, delayed marriage, the death of a spouse, and the desire to remain single. Women who have never married, however, face a number of challenges in having enough retirement income. They aren't eligible for spousal benefits from another person's pension or Social Security. They will need to live off of their own savings if income from an employer-sponsored retirement plan or their Social Security benefits isn't enough.

According to a study conducted by MetLife and the Society of Actuaries, singles are the least prepared group of all for retirement. In addition, a July 2012 US Government Accountability Office study showed that women of retirement age are twice as likely as men to live in poverty.

Single women are highly likely to become caregivers for aging parents, which can essentially end up costing a great deal of time and money. According to the MetLife Study of Caregiving Costs to Working Caregivers, males who leave the workforce early or reduce their working hours in order to provide care for a loved one lose an average of $89,000 or more in cumulative wages. Over time, this can equate to lost Social Security benefits in excess of $144,000. For women, the financial impact is substantially higher. Given an estimated loss of wages of nearly $142,700, coupled with lost Social Security benefits of roughly $131,350 and a $50,000 impact on retirement savings, a woman's average overall cost of providing care can be roughly $325,000!

With this in mind, a single woman should consider long-term care insurance for her parents as well as for themselves. In terms of harnessing guaranteed lifetime income, a lifetime income annuity can alleviate the fear of outliving their savings.

Divorced Women

Today, approximately 11 percent of women who are age 65 and over are divorced. Provided that these women have not remarried,

119

they face many of the same challenges that single women do in terms of longevity and long-term care needs.

Divorced women do, however, have some advantages in terms of income. For example, a divorced single woman may be eligible for Social Security benefits based on her ex-spouse's work record – even if her ex has remarried – provided that she is at least age 62 and:

- The marriage lasted at least ten years.
- Her ex is entitled to either Social Security retirement or disability benefits.
- The benefit that her ex is entitled to receive based on the ex's own work record is less than the benefit that she would receive based on her work record.

After receiving Social Security divorced spouse's benefits for several years, she could switch over to her own higher benefit when she turns 70. A divorced woman may also be receiving some amount of alimony from her ex-spouse to add to her income sources.

Widowed Women

Since women typically outlive men, there are a large number of widows today. In fact, 85 percent of women over age 85 are widows, compared with only 45 percent of men in that same age category.

Unfortunately, many couples fail to realize that there is a substantial decline in lifestyle at the time of widowhood. With periods of widowhood lasting 15 years or longer, widowed women don't necessarily live those years in a healthy state. According to the Society of Actuaries, 30 percent of the residual life expectancy at age 65 for women is spent in a state of chronic disability.

Older women are much more apt to have a longer period requiring assistance from some type of caregiver, whether in a facility or at home. In either case, this care can be extremely expensive. In 2013, the average private room in a nursing home in New York City cost $15,000 per month, while round-the-clock home care, at $500 per day, could reach about the same amount.

Because many women may lose a significant portion of their pension income at the death of their spouse, getting the money to pay for this care can be difficult. Proper planning must be done so that both members of a couple will receive enough income to sustain them after one has passed away.

Married Women

Even with a spouse, married women can face challenges in maximizing retirement income. Although married individuals are typically eligible to receive spousal benefits from pensions and Social Security, proper planning still must take place in order to ensure that income doesn't drop significantly at one spouse's death, leaving the other suddenly – and unexpectedly – destitute. Married women need to maximize their benefits when viewed over their potentially longer life expectancy.

When retiring, couples need to understand that one of the spouses will likely outlive the other for an extended period of time. The chance that both members of a 65-year-old couple will die within one year of each other is 3 percent; for nearly 75 percent of couples, one spouse will outlive the other by at least five years, and, for half of these couples, one will outlive the other by ten years or more. In most of these cases, the wife lives longer. Couples need to be aware that there are financial products that can provide an income "safety net" upon the death of the first spouse.

Underestimating the risk of one spouse living longer can result in an inadequate amount of continued retirement income and a drastically reduced standard of living for the surviving spouse. In order to compensate for this, couples need to plan ahead for a potential loss of income at the first spouse's death.

Women Business Owners

Over the past several years, there has been a tremendous growth of women-owned businesses. It is estimated that, today, there are roughly 10 million businesses in the United States that are majority owned by women, which represents an increase of 44 percent between 1997 and 2007 – a growth rate of twice that of male-owned businesses.

Even though many of these female business owners are savvy and successful, a large number face more financial risks and challenges than their male counterparts, especially when it comes to retirement. Longer life spans, along with the higher likelihood of disabling health conditions, can create significant financial challenges for all women, including business owners.

Only about two-thirds of women business owners have estimated how much they will need in retirement; these women can take advantage of retirement plans such as SEP IRAs, SIMPLE IRAs, and others, depending on the type and size of their business, in order to boost their retirement savings. Even with the array of savings plans available to them, only about 23 percent of women business owners have a formal, written plan for managing income and expenses in retirement. Because of this, women business owners need guidance and professional financial advice in order to reach their retirement income goals.

IDENTIFYING THE SOLUTIONS

Now that we know the problems, what are the solutions? In his report, Babbel writes that there are only three basic ways to invest your retirement money.

The first way is to annuitize a significant portion of your retirement money, thus ensuring that you will have income guaranteed for life. You must then invest the rest in a diversified portfolio to provide inflation protection. This may give some upside potential to your funds but, more importantly, you protect yourself from the downside of the market right at the time that people can least handle this risk.

Secondly, you could invest in conservative fixed interest investments, like CDs or government bonds. However, we are currently at 45-year lows in interest rates. Since these products do not offer any retirement alpha (ie, longevity credits), it will take a much larger portion of your funds to generate the same amount of income. You also *increase* the odds that you will eventually run out of money – if things don't go as planned, and many times they don't, people start tapping into their principal, which can then be quickly depleted.

The third way to invest your retirement money is to "roll the dice" and invest the entire amount in the market. However, the distribution phase is very different than the accumulation phase, and you are subject to what Babbel refers to as "reverse dollar cost averaging." Reverse dollar cost averaging is simply order of returns risk – it isn't just the long-term average market returns that matter, but the timing of those returns. In other words, what happens in the market during those first couple of years immediately before and immediately after you retire can have a much bigger impact on your overall retirement lifestyle than your average market return throughout your entire accumulation period.

Babbel also states in his report that economists the world over now agree that a significant portion of a person's retirement savings should be invested in annuities. He laments the bad press that annuities have received over the years, but he also clarifies that almost all of the press attacks have been focused on deferred annuities and not on lifetime income annuities. In fact, the press has been highly supportive of them.

KEY CHAPTER POINTS

- Women are subject to more financial risks than men overall, especially in their later years.
- The riskiest time to invest your money is the five or six years before retirement and the five or six years after retirement. Losing money within this window of time can devastate your entire retirement.
- American women face five significant hurdles that can have a major impact on retirement income.
- Roughly 75 percent of the residents of nursing homes are women.
- Less than 10 percent of women have a companion by the time their own health declines, so they need to seek institutional care.
- Women are more likely to work in part-time jobs and therefore don't qualify for an employer-sponsored retirement plan.
- Women are much less risk tolerant than men when it comes to investing.
- Most women will face certain challenges when it comes to ensuring enough income in retirement, given that all women are subject to potentially longer life expectancy, which magnifies all of the other financial risks in retirement.
- Singles are the least prepared group of all for retirement and are also most likely to become caregivers for aging parents, which can cost them a great deal in terms of time and money.
- Women of retirement age are twice as likely as men to live in poverty.

- Eighty-five percent of women over age 85 are widows, compared with only 45 percent of men in that same age category.
- Underestimating the risk of one spouse living longer than the other can result in an inadequate amount of continued retirement income and a drastically reduced standard of living for the surviving spouse.
- Couples whose marriages are not legally recognized must plan accordingly so that both partners have enough lifetime income.
- Only about 23 percent of women business owners have a formal, written plan for managing income and expenses in retirement.
- According to David Babbel, there are really only three ways to invest your retirement money: (1) Annuitize a significant portion of it and invest the rest to protect against inflation, (2) Invest in conservative fixed interest investments, or (3) Just "roll the dice" and invest the entire amount in the market.
- Economists worldwide now agree that a significant portion of a person's retirement savings should be invested in annuities.

Retirement Issues for Non-Traditional Couples

While every couple must take a number of steps to ensure a successful retirement, those in the LGBT (lesbian, gay, bisexual, transgender) community may need to take additional measures to be guaranteed that they and their partner or spouse are taken care of in their later years.

While the financial planning does not differ, the reasons why financial planning for LGBT partners may be different stems from one primary factor: the debate over their ability to legally marry a person of the same sex.

In 1996, Congress passed the federal Defense Of Marriage Act, or DOMA. This act stated the following:

> *"In determining the meaning of any Act of Congress, or of any ruling, regulation, or interpretation of the various administrative bureaus and agencies of the United States, the word 'marriage' means only a legal union between one man and one woman as husband and wife, and the word 'spouse' refers only to a person of the opposite sex who is a husband and wife."*

The law allowed states to deny marriage-type relationships for same-sex couples, even if the relationships were recognized in other states. Although the couple may have been married under the state's law, they were not considered married for federal purposes.

In January 2004, a United States Government Accountability Office report identified more than 1,100 federal statutes in which marital status was a factor in determining or receiving federal benefits, privileges, or rights. Benefits such as Social Security spousal or survivor's benefits, for instance, that were granted to legally married opposite-sex couples were not granted to married same-sex couples, even if both partners were fully insured and had paid into the Social Security program.

On June 26, 2013, however, the Supreme Court ruled that the Defense of Marriage Act was unconstitutional. Same-sex couples who were legally married in states that recognized same-sex marriage, plus Washington, DC, could be entitled to federal benefits, such as:

- Social Security retirement, spousal, survivor, and death benefits
- Survivor benefits from company pension plans
- Tax-free spousal health insurance benefits
- Estate and gift tax marital deductions
- Guaranteed leave under the Family and Medical Leave Act
- COBRA spousal health insurance coverage
- Spousal IRA rollover rights

Same-sex couples now have the right to file joint federal income tax returns. Therefore, many of the benefits that were once denied to same-sex married couples may now be, or soon become, available.

Even though there are many changes taking place, it is still extremely important to keep a close eye on planning, as not all of these changes are taking place across the board.

KEY RETIREMENT BENEFITS THAT MAY BE AFFECTED BY THE OVERTURNING OF DOMA

Just like for anyone else, retirement is a financial concern for those in the LGBT community. One area that makes this more difficult for this community is the fact that, until recently, the federal government failed to recognize same-sex marriages. Currently, there are 19 states that allow same-sex marriage, with more likely to continue passing legislation as time goes by. In these 19 states, legally married LGBT couples may be eligible for federal benefits that were once only available to opposite-sex couples.

Social Security

Following the June 2013 ruling on DOMA, Social Security can now recognize same-sex marriages for the purpose of determining entitlement to or eligibility for benefits. Same-sex spouses can now receive Social Security spousal benefits (50 percent of a worker-spouse's benefit), survivor's benefits, and the $255 lump sum death benefit payment.

The Social Security Administration is encouraging anyone in a same-sex marriage or other legal same-sex relationship to apply for benefits.

Supplemental Security Income (SSI)

Social Security is now considering same-sex marriages when processing claims for Supplemental Security Income. SSI is an income stipend for lower-income individuals who are age 65 or over, blind or disabled.

Medicare

As a result of the new DOMA legislation, the Social Security Administration is now able to process Special Enrollment Period requests for Medicare for certain individuals based on the current employment of a same-sex spouse.

When it comes to any type of government benefits, however,

it is important to be careful and not to assume anything because there are many changes still taking place with many more still to come.

RETIREMENT INCOME PLANNING FOR LGBT PARTNERS

Regardless of whether or not a couple is considered legally married, there are a number of ways to protect retirement income for a partner. Various planning methods can be used in order to maximize income, reduce taxes and transfer wealth in order to preserve as much of the estate as possible.

One of the best ways for same-sex couples (legally married or not) to ensure income for both partners is through an annuity, which provides a guaranteed income stream that cannot be outlived by either of the partners. Using the joint and survivor income payout option, there is no requirement that both income recipients need to be either legally married or related, unlike most defined-benefit pension plans that require a legally married spouse.

Another benefit is that joint and survivor annuities can avoid probate. Because wills of decedents in the LGBT community are sometimes contested by blood relatives, this can be an ideal way to protect a partner's income and reduce the possibility of a will contest. The benefits of income tax deferral on the growth of annuity funds can be an extra added bonus.

WEALTH TRANSFER FOR SAME-SEX COUPLES

Just as it is for opposite-sex married couples, the reduction or elimination of estate taxes should be a key part of planning for same-sex couples, as should the transfer of wealth with the least amount of tax ramifications. Life insurance can be a helpful tool to achieve this wealth transfer.

For couples whose marriages are not legally recognized, the unlimited marital deduction is not available upon the death of the first partner. This can mean fairly large tax consequences at the death of both partners, essentially putting the couple in double jeopardy when it comes to taxation. This can lead to an ultimate loss of assets unless proper planning is done in advance.

Life insurance can also be used as an income replacement tool, provided that there is an insurable interest between the partners. As a couple approaches retirement, it will be important to determine how sources of income will continue. For example, when one partner or spouse passes away, how will the other be affected? If income will be dramatically altered, it could require that a life insurance policy be put into place in order to replace that lost income stream for the surviving partner.

ADDITIONAL GUIDANCE

For many years, those in the LGBT market either received improper financial advice or had to more or less "wing it" when it came to setting up investment and income planning. Over time, however, a number of financial professionals have begun focusing on this particular market.

In 2011, the College for Financial Planning began offering the Accredited Domestic Partnership Advisor (ADPA) designation. This accreditation focuses on wealth transfers, federal tax issues, retirement planning, and planning for both financial and medical end-of-life needs for domestic partners. Designees must also complete 16 hours of continuing education every two years.

Anyone who is in the LGBT community and who is seeking financial or retirement planning advice would be well served to seek out a financial professional who has earned the ADPA designation.

KEY CHAPTER POINTS

- Members of the LGBT community must often take additional measures in order to ensure that they and their spouse or partner are taken care of in their later years.
- While the financial planning does not actually differ, the reasons why financial planning for LGBT partners has traditionally been different stems from one primary factor: the debate over their ability to legally marry a person of the same sex.
- A US Government Accountability Office report from January 2004 identified more than 1,100 federal statutes in which marital status was a factor in determining or receiving federal benefits, privileges, or rights.
- On June 26, 2013, the Supreme Court ruled that the Defense of Marriage Act was unconstitutional.
- Legally married same-sex couples are entitled to certain federal benefits as long as they live in a state that also recognizes same-sex marriage.
- One of the best ways for same-sex couples (legally married or not) to ensure income for both partners is through the use of an annuity.
- Life insurance can be used as an income replacement tool, provided that there is an insurable interest between the partners.
- Anyone who is in the LGBT community and who is seeking financial or retirement planning advice would be well served to seek out a financial professional who has earned the ADPA designation.

Utilizing "Longevity Credits" for Retirement Income

Forget about all of the chatter about which investment or which fund will return the most or which broker will charge the least amount of fees. There is a math and science behind creating the optimal amount – and length – of retirement income that a person needs.

Traditionally, money in retirement came from a well-diversified portfolio of stocks, bonds, real estate, and the other normal asset classes. People then withdrew a fixed amount from principal, dividends and interest. However, this "do it yourself" strategy is likely to fail if you live "too long," which is entirely possible with today's longevity, or if you continue to withdraw during an extended bear market.

Given the amount of uncertainty surrounding retirement income – namely, not knowing one's exact date of death, and, therefore, not knowing exactly how much income will be needed and for how long – annuitization becomes extremely important.

Any retirement income solution that doesn't include some form of guaranteed lifetime income is suboptimal, or less than what it could be, or should be.

IT REALLY DOESN'T MATTER WHAT YOUR "NUMBER" IS

Many people think that the success of their retirement is based on some "number": The bigger their number, the more opportunities they will have in retirement. Haven't you seen the ads from the big financial services firms that ask, *What's your number?* The truth is, success in retirement is more about what you do *with* that number.

Even more importantly, the real success of your retirement depends on two simple factors:

- How much guaranteed lifetime income do you have?
- Have you taken the key retirement risks off the table?

WHAT ARE THE KEY RETIREMENT RISKS?
LET ME QUICKLY REVIEW THEM:

- **INFLATION** – Inflation is one of the biggest factors that can affect the amount of income you will have in retirement. This is especially the case for retirees who are on a fixed income and who are depending on that income to make ends meet. A high amount of inflation can erode both your income and your portfolio if you don't properly plan for it.

  Even though the United States has experienced a relatively stable and low rate of inflation for the past quarter century, prices on food, gas and other necessities have continued to rise. Retirement income must rise along with these prices; otherwise your lifestyle will be drastically changed as you age.

- **DEFLATION** – Along with inflation, you also have deflation, which is triggered by a decline in the overall level of growth in the economy. Less demand translates to lower prices. Although low prices are not necessarily a bad thing, if prices are low because of lack of demand, the economy will begin to stagnate and contract.

- **WITHDRAWAL RATE** – The amount of money that you withdraw from your retirement savings, especially when factored in conjunction with your lifespan, will also be a determinant in whether or not you live comfortably in retirement. For example, if you have $1 million saved and you withdraw at a rate of 5 percent, or $50,000 per year, your money would last a lot longer than if you withdrew at a rate of 10 percent, or $100,000 per year. As discussed in Step 5, however, 5 percent is not a safe withdrawal rate.

How do you know the proper withdrawal rate? You don't, unless you know the exact year, month, and day that you are going to die; then you can calculate when it's safe to run out of money. Since you can't calculate this, the ideal income strategy includes guaranteed lifetime income.

- **ORDER OF RETURNS** – If you had money in the stock market in 2008, then you know just how quickly the market can turn. Most investors are at least somewhat aware of average return over time.

  But, on the day that you retire and start taking money out of your portfolio, average market returns don't matter nearly as much. What matters a whole lot more is what happens in those few years just prior to and just after you retire.

- **LONGEVITY, OR THE MULTIPLIER OF ALL OTHER RETIREMENT RISKS** – Everyone knows that people are living longer, which is a good thing – for the most part. But when it comes to stretching retirement income, longevity can cause issues. Income must last for a longer period of time.

  Longevity isn't just a risk in and of itself; it is a *multiplier* of all of the other retirement risks. It has the potential to stretch out all of the other risks for a longer period of time. For example, if you live longer, you'll be exposed to inflation and deflation for longer. Likewise, you'll be withdrawing money from your portfolio for a longer period of time as well, provided that there are still funds left to withdraw.

Because longevity multiplies all of the other retirement risks, it is essential that you remove this risk from the table. In doing so, you will need to transfer some – or all – of that risk to an insurance company. Why? Because insurance companies are in the business of "pooling" risk. Here's what I mean: The risk to an insurer when it sells life insurance is that someone will die too soon and a claim will have to be paid. The risk to an insurer when they sell a lifetime income annuity is that someone will live too long and they will have to pay out income for too many years. Because insurance companies are essentially on "both sides of the table," they are in a perfect position to hedge longevity risk. There is no other industry that can do this.

There are many financial professionals today who use age 90 as the maximum age for retirement income plan illustrations. I believe that they do this because their plans will not hold up much beyond that age.

Even though most people don't think that they will live to age 90, the facts are very different: 33 percent of men and 44 percent of women will live beyond age 90, and 63 percent of all married couples will have at least one of them live beyond age 90. Therefore, if you are married and set up a financial plan that will only last until age 90, that plan will fail 63 percent of the time.

PROBABILITY OF A 65-YEAR-OLD LIVING TO:

PROBABILITY	MALE	FEMALE	ONE SPOUSE
50%	85	88	92
25%	92	94	97

ACCUMULATION VERSUS DISTRIBUTION

Few financial professionals have made the transition from accumulation to distribution. They still use systematic withdrawals from diversified portfolios or bond ladders to provide retirement income. These types of investment vehicles subject their clients to market risk, interest rate risk, withdrawal risk, order of return risk, and, most significantly, longevity risk. Before you let these professionals plan your traditional retirement plan, see what the Financial Research Corporation has to say: "We have proven that even a well-constructed moderate portfolio is likely to fail over the long term if investors get aggressive with withdrawal rates as many will." What is considered aggressive? Today, a 4 percent or more withdrawal rate is!

Financial professionals have the obligation to ensure that their clients have successful outcomes, regardless of what type of economic storms they face. High inflation, market downturns, and medical advances in longevity are all examples of such storms. Here is a simple question that I have for your financial professional who wants to build you a traditional retirement plan: If they do *not* use a lifetime income annuity as a portion of the portfolio, how can they protect you from all of these potential storms? The answer is, they can't.

Most people don't realize how income annuities are able to offer such high cash flows given that they are an insurance product. These products provide investors with a type of alpha that traditional investments simply cant match: longevity credits, also known as mortality credits. This is what separates income annuities from other investment options within the fixed income market.

As discussed in Step 5, the cash flow from an income annuity comes from three different sources: interest, a return of principal,

137

and mortality credits. Traditional investments can typically manufacture two of these components – interest and return of principal – through a portfolio of bonds. However, only mortality credits can provide additional cash flow.

Mortality credits are derived from the mortality pool that is built into income annuities. Essentially, the insurance company sells annuities to thousands of investors – some of whom will die early, and some who will die later. By applying principal from those who die early to those who die late, the insurance company is able to guarantee a higher, lifelong payout to everyone, no matter how long they live.

COMPONENTS OF GUARANTEED LIFETIME INCOME PAYOUT: MALE AGE 65, $100,000 INVESTMENT

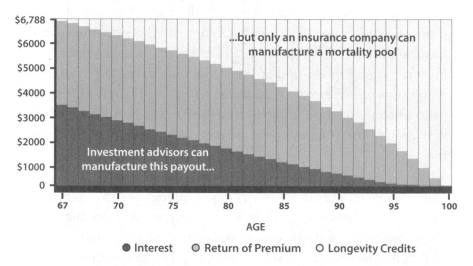

Longevity credits increase significantly with age. As people grow older, their future lifespan decreases. Older investors are more likely to return their capital to the mortality pool quickly, generating more cash flow for the remaining investors, which is why income annuity payout rates increase with age.

The payout provided by the insurance company is guaranteed, regardless of the performance of the mortality pool. Insurance companies can do this without assuming significant risk because of the law of large numbers: With thousands of investors in the pool, they can predict more or less how many investors will die each year.

Only life insurance companies can manufacture mortality credits. There is no such thing as a "synthetic" mortality credit. Just as importantly, the life insurance industry does not have an infinite capacity; there is essentially a limit on how many income annuities the entire industry can produce.

The amount of income that a retiree receives in retirement is central to how likely he or she is to succeed. While withdrawing 4 percent of one's portfolio has often worked, a lower rate could still be successful – as long as it produces enough income for a retiree to be comfortable – but a higher rate increases the risk of failure.

There's another issue, too: Having a long-term plan that relies on withdrawing only the interest or earnings, without touching any principal, could pose a considerable hazard. Why? This particular strategy may not take into account inflation or investment risk. It could influence a retiree to focus on withdrawing from investments that actually provide the highest income or returns. In addition, interest risk fluctuation over the long term may not keep this strategy sustainable. The only time this technique may work is when it funds only discretionary expenses.

HURRY, WHILE SUPPLIES LAST!

At first, I was surprised to learn that the life insurance industry has only a limited amount of mortality credits. I did not realize that the supply of lifetime income annuities is limited. Over the next decade, these products are likely to be priced very differently than they are today.

You should start by covering 100 percent of your "minimum acceptable level of retirement income" with annuities. This approach provides the most cost-effective and practical way to provide for security in retirement. After covering these basic expenses, you will need to put a significant amount of your remaining portfolio in annuities and invest some in stocks, bonds, and money market funds. In addition, I believe that extra attention needs to be paid in the optimization phase to inflation-protected investments, such as gold, silver, oil, and real estate. While these financial vehicles can complement a portfolio, stocks and bonds are no substitute for annuities.

According to Moshe A. Milevsky, one of the modern day heroes of retirement income, "very few people actually annuitize their wealth even though countless studies have shown that this is exactly what they should do." Today, many economists, including some Nobel Prize winners, are in agreement that annuities are the best way to optimize one's retirement income.

KEY CHAPTER POINTS

- There is a math and science behind creating the optimum amount and length of retirement income that a person needs.
- The "do it yourself" retirement income strategy is likely to fail if you live "too long," which is entirely possible today.
- Given the amount of uncertainty surrounding retirement today, any retirement income solution that doesn't include at least some form of guaranteed lifetime income is suboptimal, or less than it could be, or should be.
- Success in retirement is less about what your number is and more about what you do with that number.
- Thirty-three percent of men and 44 percent of women will live beyond age 90, and 63 percent of all married couples will have at least one of them live beyond age 90.

- Few financial professionals have made the transition from accumulation to distribution.
- Even a well-constructed moderate portfolio is likely to fail over the long term if investors get aggressive with withdrawal rates, as many will.
- Insurance companies can guarantee the payout without assuming significant risk because of the law of large numbers.
- Income annuity payout rates increase with age.
- Only life insurance companies can manufacture mortality credits.
- There is a limit on how many income annuities the life insurance industry can produce.
- The amount of income that a retiree receives in retirement is central to how likely they are to succeed.
- While various financial vehicles can complement a portfolio, stocks and bonds are no substitute for annuities.

What Does Life Insurance Have To Do with Retirement?

People may think life insurance has nothing to do with retirement but, the truth is, life insurance has *everything* to do with it! The people who enter retirement with a significant amount of permanent life insurance will likely enjoy a much happier and more successful retirement than those who don't.

However, many seniors are living a "just in case" retirement. One of the key elements of this deals with leaving a legacy to children. The parents live a diminished retirement because they want to "leave something for the kids." They don't spend their money, and then what happens? They die. What happens to the money? It goes to their kids, who then use it for the reasons their parents were saving it for – a new boat, a cruise, the country club, etc. On the other hand, many people have told me that they don't believe they need to leave their kids anything. Then why do so many people refuse to spend their retirement assets? This retirement paradox can be solved with life insurance.

When you ask most people how much money they want to leave their children or grandchildren, many of them say, "Well, I guess whatever is left over…" Is this the most efficient way to transfer assets? No. If you decide up front how much to leave the kids, then, for pennies on the dollar, you can use the money from life insurance to go to the kids, both income tax and estate tax free. You get the leverage of mortality credits offered by the life insurance policy. Then you can buy guaranteed lifetime income – receiving dollars for pennies from the mortality credits offered by the annuity!

Life insurance and guaranteed lifetime income are tied together: This is the new "retirement alpha" that is the key to retirement success.

143

LIFE INSURANCE AND RETIREMENT ALPHA

When I first heard about retirement alpha through the Financial Research Corporation of Boston white paper, the concept rocked my world. Alpha is a form of outperformance of an investment. People are not getting any alpha from their CDs or bonds; their stock portfolios do not give them consistent or reliable alpha; and the sequence of returns could wipe them out if they withdraw money during a down market—this new retirement alpha is the way to go!

I once heard a speaker at a LIMRA conference who opened my eyes to required minimum distributions (RMDs). He said: "Does everyone realize that RMDs were never created to give clients income in retirement? They were created solely as a tax recapture plan for the federal government!" Because you get a tax deduction and a tax deferral when you put money into an individual retirement account (IRA) or 401(k), the only way the government could get taxes on that money was to establish the RMD. Yet, many seniors use it for their retirement income.

RMD maximization the strategy I use to help seniors get the most after-tax income by optimizing the RMDs that they must start taking at age 70½.

For example, a husband and wife have a total of $250,000 in IRA money. Since they are both age 70½, they need to start taking their required minimum distributions. The RMD starts at about $9,000 and climbs each year, topping out at about $13,000 when the clients are in their nineties. If they live too long, the RMDs start dropping rapidly until the client is nearly out of money – by age 110 or so. This scenario is suboptimal.

Let me explain what I mean by "suboptimal." When I ask, "Why are you saving money in an IRA or 401(k)? What are you saving it for?," they obviously respond, "For retirement." When you are 70½, you are in retirement. If you are 70½, when do you think your best ten years in retirement will be? And I always hear, "My next ten years," or from age 70 to 80.

TURN RMDs INTO INCOME FOR LIFE

If you have an IRA or other qualified savings plan, you'll have to start taking Required Minimum Distributions (RMDs), or mandatory withdrawals, from that account once you reach age 70½ *

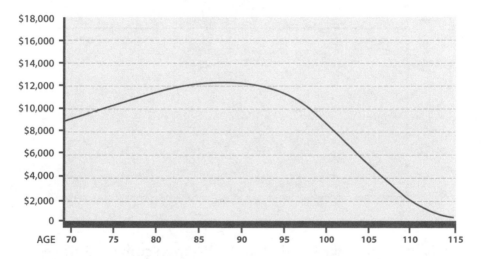

- RMDs can be a chore to keep track of, especially if you have more than one IRA or qualified account.

- Your required withdrawal amount will be different each year. They will increase over time and then decrease later in life.

- You also may have to complete withdrawal forms, or other administrative paperwork each year. Additionally, there is a 50% penalty if you fail to take out the correct amount.

However, during your best ten years, the government has you taking out the least. When you are in your nineties, you take out the *most* mandatory withdrawals. If you live too long, this starts heading rapidly toward zero! This is not an optimal retirement plan.

A LIFETIME INCOME ANNUITY CAN HELP MAXIMIZE YOUR RETIREMENT INCOME WHILE SATISFYING IRS RMD RULES,*

There is a simpler and more advantageous way to satisfy your RMDs—roll your qualified money into an immediate Annuity.

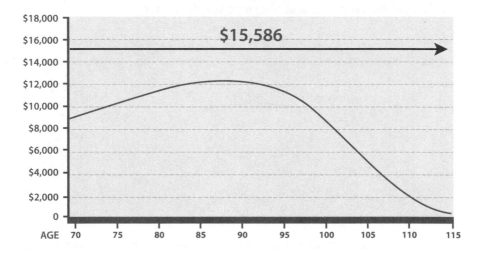

- Satisfy your annual distribution requirements (if properly structured).

- Receive greater income than you would from RMDs.

- Eliminate the need to complete annual withdrawal paperwork.

- Receive a guaranteed income for the rest of your life or spread payments over two lives using the Joint Life option.

- Reduce your tax burden by spreading it over a lifetime of payments.

A joint lifetime income annuity with cash refund allows the husband from our example to receive the same amount of money the whole time. He'll get a check for the rest of his life, then, when he dies, the wife gets a check for the rest of her life, and, if they both die, the kids are protected by the cash refund feature.

Many people don't believe that you can do joint life on an IRA, but you can! You can do joint life with your spouse, joint life with your kids, you could even do joint life with your golfing buddy. For our current example, the husband picked his wife. How many years in a row, under the current assumptions, does the lifetime income annuity pay more than the RMD? Every single year. It's an overall win: You get more during your best ten years, and the income is predictable and dependable.

While most people love this concept, some will hesitate over the tax issue. I'll usually hear something like this: "Well, Tom, I don't even like getting that RMD money because I have to pay taxes, and I hate paying taxes. All you're doing is sending me *more* money. That just means I have to pay more in taxes, and I just told you how much I hate to pay taxes!"

When you take your RMD, where do you pay your taxes from? From your RMD, and you're left with an amount less than your RMD. But you don't have to do that anymore. With a lifetime income annuity, you get more money so that you are still left with more after taxes than what you would with an RMD. In effect, you are using the longevity credits to pay the taxes.

I am not arguing that taxes don't matter. It is where you can get the most amount of money *after* taxes that really counts. Even if it didn't pay more, the stability and predictability of income from a lifetime income annuity makes it more desirable for a retiree.

DO YOU REALLY NEED LIFE INSURANCE IN RETIREMENT?

Many people argue that they don't *need* any of that money. I say to that, If you don't *need* this money, then, what do you *want* this money to do when you die?

When they say they'll leave it to the kids, I remind them that this may not be a smart option: Income taxes, estate taxes, and income in respect of a decedent can wipe out 50 percent or more of that money! It may be better to use this money to pay for life insurance premiums for a policy that could go income and estate tax free to their family. This is how you supercharge the RMD maximization idea.

Another technique is RMD compression. For those who don't want their RMDs and have no one to give them to, they can put an inflation rider on the lifetime income annuity. I recommend the highest inflation protection the company will allow, which can "compress" the RMDs for about eight years. Over time, the lifetime income annuity payments will increase and, depending on how long the person lives, will pay significantly more money. Some people find this attractive.

A recent Treasury ruling now allows you to use your IRA or 401(k) money to purchase a Deferred Income Annuity called a Qualified Longevity Annuity Contract, or QLAC. With this option, you do not have to withdraw RMDs on the money you put into the deferred income annuity *even if* the income starts after age 70 ½! Yet, you're still able to hedge the risk of drawing down your benefits too quickly and thereby outliving your retirement savings. Be ready to see many creative ways to use this ruling.

You have many options (that most people have no idea about) when it comes to required minimum distributions. So let's move on to some other ways to use life insurance in retirement.

LIFE INSURANCE AS A LEGACY FOR GRANDCHILDREN

Even if some retirees don't want to leave their children any money, many want to do something for their grandchildren. They are concerned about the economy and their grandchildren's future. They want to help provide a college education or money for that first house.

Case Study

Consider Annie. Annie is 62 years old and has four children, all grown and married, with six grandkids. While her estate is set to be divided equally among her children, she wants to leave each grandchild a comfortable sum of money. Annie has a $100,000 CD that she doesn't need for retirement income, which she plans to use to fund legacy gifts for her grandchildren. The $100,000 grows at a hypothetical 2 percent annually, and Annie will pay taxes on this gain each year. Upon her death, the balance will be divided equally among her grandchildren.

After speaking with her financial professional, Annie discovered an option that would allow her to instantly double what her grandchildren would receive today and establish a greater legacy well into the future. By putting the $100,000 into a permanent life insurance policy, she would no longer have to pay taxes on her CD interest each year. She also immediately turns the $100,000 asset into $220,000 in guaranteed death benefit that would be passed generally income tax free to her grandchildren as beneficiaries.

Annie can choose to purchase six individual policies with each grandchild designated the sole beneficiary or she can purchase a single policy with six equal beneficiaries. Best of all, when a new grandchild is born, she has the option to either purchase an additional policy or simply add the child as a beneficiary to the existing policy, effectively dividing the face value of the policy seven ways.

As far as giving up liquidity in case of an emergency, many life insurance policies offer significant liquidity – some even offer a full money back guarantee at any time! If you are trying to give your grandchildren a head start in life, I recommend this option.

LIFE INSURANCE FOR CHARITABLE GIVING

Many retirees have philanthropic wishes. They want to leave money to their church, university, or favorite charity. Life insurance can allow you to leave even more to your cause.

Case Study

Al and Helen, ages 64 and 61, have more than enough money to live a comfortable retirement and would like to give $50,000 to charity. The more they discuss it, the more they realize that they would each like to give $50,000 to different charities. How can you each give $50,000 if all you have is $50,000? Life insurance.

After meeting with their financial professional, Al and Helen discover that a permanent life insurance policy may provide the answer to their dilemma. The couple splits their $50,000 savings and purchases two individual policies, each with a life insurance benefit of $50,000 for a total gift of $100,000.
Al and Helen maintain control over both policies throughout their lives, thus preserving their flexibility to change beneficiaries, or, if they have a need, to cancel their policies with the access to their surrender values. Best of all, Al and Helen were able to double their capacity to make a charitable gift and grant legacy gifts to both of their favorite charities.

USING LIFE INSURANCE TO COVER FINAL EXPENSES

Many seniors want to avoid being a financial burden to their children when they die, especially since funeral expenses have soared over the years. According to the National Funeral Directors Association, the average cost of a funeral in 2013, including the gravesite and vault, was nearly $10,000 but can be a lot more, depending on the services. Try watching television without seeing an ad about prepaid funeral services.

Case Study

John and Leslie have been enjoying their retirement. They have a sound financial plan that includes a modest inheritance for their children, but they remain concerned about leaving a financial burden upon their death. They know that the $10,000 they have each set aside to cover their final expenses may be insufficient, but they don't have any other money to put toward this. They would like a way to cover their final expenses without having their children use their inheritance to cover these costs. Unsure of what to do, they look to their financial professional for guidance.

Their financial professional suggests that they each purchase a permanent life insurance policy. When either of them passes away, it will provide a leveraged death benefit that can be used to help cover their final expenses, thereby keeping their children's inheritance intact. Best of all, Leslie and John will maintain control over both policies throughout their lives. They can change beneficiaries or exercise the policies' surrender values should their needs change. By splitting their $20,000 savings and purchasing two individual life insurance policies, they have a total of $32,600 in death benefit.

USING LIFE INSURANCE TO PROTECT
SOCIAL SECURITY BENEFITS

As we discussed in the chapter about Social Security, many people don't fully understand how Social Security works. When a husband or wife dies, one of the Social Security checks dies as well. Whichever spouse's check was higher, that check will continue to go to the surviving spouse. However, the lower check will stop, causing problems for the surviving spouse.

Conventional wisdom says that a young family needs life insurance on a working spouse to help replace the lost income if the spouse dies unexpectedly. What about life insurance to replace retirement income that will cease at the death of a spouse, such as Social Security?

- Permanent cash value life insurance can provide cash at death (generally income tax free) to provide income for the surviving spouse.
- People age 60+ are the fastest growing segment buying new life insurance policies.
- Premiums for life insurance are higher after age 60 than for people in their thirties or forties. This is why you should consider permanent life insurance earlier.
- Many people buy permanent life insurance while they are still working, knowing that the cash value or death benefit can be used when they retire to help replace the lost income from Social Security or another source.

Let's take a practical look at life insurance. Think about your key ring; what is on it? Your car keys – you have automobile insurance. Your house key – you have homeowners insurance. What about you? What are *you* worth.

Pretend you had a machine in your garage that kicked out $5,000 a month for 40 years. What would that machine be worth? Would you secure that machine? If you could buy insurance for it would you? How much? Guess what? YOU are that miracle money machine!

Throughout your life, you are going to earn a fortune. Your total economic wealth is made up of two parts – human capital and financial capital. The present value of all of your future earnings is called your human capital. Many times, financial professionals only want to talk to people about their financial capital. However, your human capital may be even more valuable. If you only focus on financial capital, when someone dies, there will be a huge loss of future earnings. When calculating your total net worth, don't forget about your human capital!

For the young people reading this book – you may not have much money now, but your human capital could be worth millions of dollars! That is why it is so important for young people to have life insurance. No other financial product can protect your human capital. There is no stock or bond that will instantly be worth $3,000,000 upon your death. A life insurance policy can do that. Similar to lifetime income annuities being the only product that can guarantee income for the rest of your life, life insurance is the only product that can protect your human capital if you die too soon. These are unique products in the financial world.

LIFE INSURANCE IS A WOMEN'S ISSUE

Seventy percent of married baby boomer women will become widows. Because women live longer and typically marry men older than themselves, they may be widows for 10, 20, or even 30 years. A woman's retirement is an important topic that many people are talking about. I wrote an article about why people, especially women, would continue to buy life insurance despite the terrible market of 2008, and I recently spoke to the National Association of Homebuilders about "What Women Want in Retirement."

With the recent drop in markets and housing, many of the baby boomer men are underinsured. Who will pay the consequences? Women! Don't take my word for it: Find a widow who is living well and a widow who isn't. Ask them about the importance of life insurance – it will be the key difference between them.

LIFE INSURANCE IS A TAX ISSUE AS WELL

We all know the importance of asset allocation and diversification of investments among stocks, bonds, commodities and cash, or the "don't put all of your eggs in one basket" mindset. By diversifying your assets, you balance the ups and downs since, historically, not all asset classes move up or down together. However, more recently, all of *these* assets have gone up or down together, so the search for non-correlated assets continues to be a very important part of asset diversification.

What about tax diversification? Most people have the majority of their assets in "qualified" or "pre-tax" accounts such as 401(k) s, tax-sheltered annuity plans (TSAs), and IRAs. These vehicles offer tremendous tax advantages in the accumulation phase: The contributions are often tax deductible and they offer tax-deferred growth. However, in the distribution phase, they can be a tax nightmare since all distributions are fully taxable. With the economic problems facing this country, where do you think tax rates are going? The math is clear – taxes will be going up. I have no doubt about that.

If you agree with that proposition, my question is this: How much sense is it to have all or most of your money in fully taxable accounts? Wouldn't it be better to have some of that money invested where withdrawals would be tax free?

If you could invest in the "tax perfect" retirement plan, what would it look like? It would probably include:

1. Contributions that are tax deductible
2. Accumulation that is tax deferred
3. Distributions that are tax free

Unfortunately, such a plan does not exist. But you can get either 1 & 2 or 2 & 3.

Most people select 1 & 2: the IRA, 401(k), TSA, 403(b), and pension plans. You get a deduction when you put the money in, it grows tax deferred, and you pay taxes when you take it out.

Many people increasingly like the idea of 2 & 3 – paying taxes now on savings for retirement, knowing that they will not have to pay taxes on the growth or on the distribution of that savings. The most common financial vehicles that do that are the Roth IRA, tax-free municipal bonds, and cash value life insurance.

A TAX PERFECT PLAN DOES NOT EXIST, BUT YOU MAY BE ABLE TO GET 1&2 OR 2&3

1. Contributions that are tax deductible	**2.** Accumulation that is tax deferred	**3.** Distributions that are tax free

1. Contributions	Tax-Deductible	After-Tax
2. Accumulations	Tax-Deferred	Tax Deferred
3. Distributions	Taxable	Tax-Free

Financial Vehicles	• Traditional IRA • 401(k) plan • Pension plan • Profit-sharing plan • Keogh plan	• Roth IRA • Tax-free municipal bond • Cash Value Life Insurance

Imagine you are a farmer – would you rather pay tax on the seed or on the harvest? Almost every farmer would rather pay tax on the seed. It works the same way with money. Putting money in a Roth IRA or cash value life insurance is paying tax on the seed. Putting money into 401(k)s and traditional IRAs is paying tax on the harvest.

Although I am a big supporter of Roth IRAs, they do not allow unlimited contributions. Tax-free bonds can work, too, but be very careful since states and municipalities are having significant financial issues. Additionally, as interest rates rise, the value of the bonds will go down.

Permanent life insurance that builds cash value can be a great tool in this situation. The premiums are paid with after-tax dollars. The policy grows tax deferred, and you can access those cash values before or after retirement on a tax-free basis as long as it is structured properly. Upon your death, the death benefit is paid to your beneficiaries generally income tax free and, if you set it up properly, estate tax free.

Example

You are taking $100,000 in income from tax qualified savings, such as a 401(k) or IRA. Under today's tax brackets, if there was no additional income, you would be in a 25 percent tax bracket, resulting in a $25,000 tax (assuming no deductions for the sake of simplicity). That leaves $75,000 to spend after taxes.

If, for instance, we took $50,000 from a totally taxable qualified plan and $50,000 from a tax-free bucket of money, there would be no tax on half and a 15% tax bracket on the other half that we do have to pay taxes on. That leaves us over $92,500 to spend! By employing a tax diversification strategy and moving a portion of your money into a cash value life insurance, you can lower your taxes, giving yourself more to spend and allowing you to increase your standard of living.

LIFE INSURANCE IS A WEALTH TRANSFER ISSUE

Why do the wealthiest people in America buy the biggest life insurance policies? It isn't because they need it. They have plenty of money. Their kids will have plenty of money. Why buy it? It is because they want to leave their money an efficient way!

There are only three things that will happen to your money and assets when you die:

1. It will go to your family.
2. It will go to charity.
3. It will go to the IRS.

You need to think about where you want your money to go when you die. Right now, for the wealthiest Americans, their largest heir is the IRS. It doesn't matter how much money you have – the majority of people are not comfortable leaving the IRS more money than will be going to each of their children. That is why wealthy people buy life insurance. Using life insurance is, for many people, the most efficient way to transfer wealth to heirs. But remember, you need to take into account your personal facts and circumstances.

With life insurance, you gain tremendous leverage. Depending on your age, sex and health, instead of leaving someone $100,000, you could put that $100,000 into a life insurance policy and leave them $200,000, $300,000, or even $500,000. Second, and maybe best of all, it will normally go income tax free. Third, if you set it up properly, you can even leave the money estate tax free as well. Finally, money left via life insurance is completely private – there is no probate! It will not get published in the local papers like money that's left in a will.

Many of you think that this doesn't apply to you because you don't have to worry about estate taxes, at least not right now. The current estate tax doesn't even kick in until $5.34 million for an individual and $10.68 million for a couple.

Well, what if you could leave your family $20,000 or $30,000 instead of the $10,000 you were planning? What if you could leave a grandchild more money to help them with their college education or buying a first home? There are many reasons why regular people use life insurance in retirement. Additionally, just because the current estate tax exemptions are so high doesn't mean they will stay there.

Year	Estate Tax Exemption	Top Estate Tax Rate
1997	$600,000	55%
1998	$625,000	55%
1999	$650,000	55%
2000	$675,000	55%
2001	$675,000	55%
2002	$1,000,000	50%
2003	$1,000,000	49%
2004	$1,500,000	48%
2005	$1,500,000	47%
2006	$2,000,000	46%
2007	$2,000,000	45%
2008	$2,000,000	45%
2009	$3,500,000	45%
2010	Unlimited	0%
2011	$5,000,000	35%
2012	$5,000,000	35%
2013	$5,250,000	55%
2014	$5,340,000	55%

Just look at this chart to see how estate taxes have been a political football over the years

Case Study

I have worked with many wealthy people over the years. Whenever we get to the estate planning portion of the discussion, clients have a tough time understanding why they should buy a large life insurance policy.

A financial professional had called me in on an appointment with a very successful rancher in Sterling, Colorado. The financial professional was recommending a $7 million life insurance policy to pay the estate taxes, but the rancher was sitting there with his arms crossed. "I don't want or need life insurance!" he said. "Heck, I'm loaded – I'm worth $15 million. Life insurance is the last thing I need. I think you boys are just trying to make a big commission."

I didn't even flinch – this is a very common objection from wealthy people. In fact, I smiled because I knew it was coming. I leaned forward, looked him in the eyes, and said, "Let me be the first to agree with you. You are worth a lot of money and you are correct – you don't need any life insurance in the traditional sense. Your family will be fine financially whether you live or die. However, what you need is a way to transfer your wealth to your children and grandchildren in the most tax-efficient manner possible. If we could transfer your wealth with stocks or bonds or real estate, we would. But it just so happens that life insurance is the most efficient wealth transfer vehicle because of the tax advantages and the leverage it gives you. So, I completely agree that you don't need life insurance, but you do need a wealth transfer vehicle. That just happens to be life insurance." This answer works with most people. But not that day. He crossed his arms again. "Boys, there will be no life insurance purchased here today. I might have been born at night but it was not LAST NIGHT."

At this point, the financial professional reached into his bag and took out four plastic cows from a kid's farming set. He set them on the table. "These are your four cash cows. This one represents all of your land. This one represents all of your buildings. This one represents all of your equipment, and this one represents all of your investments and bank accounts. Now, what Tom was trying to say is that when you die, the IRS is going to come to the farm and butcher two of these cows." At the time, the estate tax was about 50 percent after very low exemptions. "They will butcher those two cows and keep all of the meat. All Tom was recommending is that instead of butchering those two cows, instead, we take a little milk from each of the four cows. The milk is used to buy a policy. When you die, the policy goes to the IRS and your family gets to keep your four cash cows. Now, one of those two things IS going to happen – but you get to pick which one."

A light bulb went on in his head. "Heck," he said. "Every rancher knows it is better to give up a little milk than to butcher two good cows!" While neither the attorney nor I could explain estate planning to him, the rancher understood those toy cows! I learned a lot that day about storytelling and the power of simplicity.

THE ULTIMATE TRUTH ABOUT LIFE INSURANCE

I am often asked, "Which type of life insurance should I buy: Term? Whole life? Universal life? Variable life? Indexed life? Which is the best?"

Here is the ultimate truth about life insurance: The *only* policy that matters is the one that is in force on the day that you die. However, less than 2 percent of term life policies are in force on the day that you die.

While I am not against term life insurance, it is not a solution for people in retirement or for those who want to retire. Term life is for supplemental coverage while your kids are at home and you have a high mortgage or other financial obligations. It was never meant to be the only life insurance you would own.

Think of all the so called "experts" on television and on the radio who have advised millions of people to skip over permanent life insurance policies. Their advice was to "buy term and invest the difference." An entire generation bought into that opinion; however, rather than buying term and investing the difference, most bought term and spent the difference. Or even worse, they bought term and lost the difference! Now an entire generation of Americans is approaching retirement without any permanent life insurance. Where are these experts who told them that their house would be paid off (it isn't), they would have a pension (they don't), their kids would be on their own (they're not), and there would be no more need for any life insurance (but there is)?

Americans are wildly underinsured and most have no idea! This low interest rate environment has immediate impacts on your life insurance and retirement savings. I would be so bold as to say that almost every single person reading this book is currently underinsured for life insurance: In a 1 percent interest rate environment, it takes $5,000,000 of life insurance to protect every $50,000 of income. How many people do you know that make $50,000 per year and have $5,000,000 of life insurance? Not many, I'm assuming.

While some of you may think that is ridiculous, I would respond, *How much life insurance would you need to protect $50,000 of income if we were in a 5 percent interest environment?* $1,000,000 – that is not ridiculous. I firmly believe that you need to have no less than $1,000,000 of life insurance for every $50,000 of income.

Case Study

I met with a 47-year-old widow whose husband had been killed in a car accident. She was a stay-at-home mom with two young girls. After expressing my condolences, I asked her to tell me about her financial situation. She revealed that her husband had a $1,000,000 life insurance policy. She never thought she would ever be a "millionaire." She envisioned a few "wants" to use the money, including the building of a custom house on a lake.

She was absolutely shocked when I explained to her that, in this low interest rate environment, $1,000,000 would not provide that kind of lifestyle: It would only produce $10,000 of annual income (at current 1 percent interest rates). We could maybe push it to $35,000 or $38,000, but most of the research now says a 4 percent withdrawal rate will probably not survive 40 or 50 years. "But," she said, "my husband made $250,000 per year! There is no way we can live on $38,000 per year!" How could I tell her that $1,000,000 was nowhere near enough life insurance for someone making $250,000 per year?

How many people reading this book right now are in the exact same situation? I strongly recommend that you look at your own life insurance situation to see what would happen to your family if something were to happen to you.

KEY CHAPTER POINTS

- Life insurance has everything to do with retirement.
- Retirement alpha can be used in the legacy stage.
- Permanent life insurance is one of the very best wealth transfer tools available.
- Maximizing required minimum distributions can increase retirement income and create dependable, reliable income.

- You may not need life insurance in the "traditional sense" in retirement, but it can serve other purposes such as transferring assets, providing a way to leave a legacy, increasing an inheritance, donating more to charity, covering final expenses and protecting Social Security benefits for a surviving spouse.
- Life insurance can make a big difference in the life of a widow or widower.
- The cash value inside of a permanent life insurance policy grows tax deferred.
- Life insurance proceeds can pass income tax free, and they avoid probate.
- Using life insurance as an estate planning tool can help you to avoid "butchering your cash cows."
- It is absolutely crucial to ensure that you have enough life insurance.

Conclusion

There you have it – my seven steps to retirement security, along with some extra pointers. These seven steps cover the basic information that you need to secure your retirement. The extra pointers are equally important. Remember, retirement is not an end; it is a new beginning to the best years of your life. To make sure you're ready for Happily Ever After, let's briefly review some key points.

First of all, this book is based on math and science, not someone's opinions. I want you to do your due diligence on my recommendations. What you will find is that these solutions are backed by PhDs around the world. Because no one knows what the best solution will be, math and science always try to find the *optimal* solution.

Retirement today is very different than the retirement of our parents. It is up to us to figure out how to get the right amount of income – not too much that you run out, but not too little that you never enjoy the retirement you are entitled to. The ultimate success of your retirement will be about income, not assets, and how you handle risk management.

Most people underestimate their longevity. With medical advances increasing by leaps and bounds, longevity will be the number one risk that you will likely face in retirement. Stocks, bonds, and real estate just cannot take this risk off the table.

Having a plan and working with a trusted financial professional are important ways to combat risk. Retirement is *not* a "do it yourself" project. You will be happier and more confident in retirement if you have a plan. I would encourage you to go back and review the Legacy Questions that John Homer poses to his clients. I also gave you some tips on how to find a trusted financial professional. (All of this is in the Step 1 chapter.)

Since Social Security is the largest retirement asset that most people have, I explained the importance of maximizing these benefits. Do not worry: Social Security *will* be there for you. But don't rush taking it; delay your benefits because you will likely live far longer than you think, and those increased benefits will serve you well for many years. I shared some cutting-edge strategies like "file and suspend" and "filing a restricted application." (In the Step 2 chapter.)

We then discussed why working in retirement may be a good thing, not something to dread. It can keep your brain active, and having a purpose in your life is very important to living a long life and being happy. Every extra year that you work can add security to your savings, increase future Social Security benefits, and reduce the number of years you have to live off your investments. But do something you really love doing. Retirement is a time when you can focus on things that matter to you. (Step 3.)

We focused on the importance of investing some of your portfolio to protect from inflation. Inflation is like a virus that slowly but then very quickly can devastate purchasing power. You not only need income to age 100 and beyond, you need *increasing* income to age 100 and beyond! Historically, stocks, real estate, and some commodities have helped people protect their purchasing power. By having some guaranteed lifetime income in that portfolio, you are given license to take some risk with the rest of the portfolio! (Step 4.)

The next step was securing more guaranteed lifetime income. We looked at Social Security, pensions and annuities as sources of guaranteed lifetime income. These are the only sources that can take longevity risk off the table. Retirees with guaranteed lifetime income were happier and tended to live longer than those who did not. This is fact, not opinion. (Step 5.)

I adamantly stated that no retirement plan is complete without a plan for long-term care. It is the one risk that most people forget about, and it can wipe out even a very large retirement portfolio quickly. Minimize this risk by using long-term care insurance, a life insurance policy with a long-term care benefit, an annuity with a long-term care benefit, or some combination of those products. These products are being developed so rapidly, the average person cannot keep up with them, so trust a financial professional. (Step 6.)

The final step was using home equity wisely. We looked at downsizing, home equity lines of credit, and reverse mortgages. My best advice is to be very careful. Work with someone who has expertise in these areas so they can give you options and good advice. Your home may very well be the largest investment you have ever made. You want to use it wisely. (Step 7.)

We talked about being happy in retirement. You can be truly happy by having a purpose, a plan, friends, and close neighbors; accomplishing things that you have always wanted to do, whether that be traveling or picking up a special hobby; and, of course, having guaranteed lifetime income. I really cannot stress enough the importance of lifetime income to the ultimate success of your retirement and your happiness.

I shared with you how longevity credits are a new form of alpha – "Retirement Alpha." You cannot retire optimally without it. I also shared why all of the talking heads on television telling you that you won't need life insurance when you retire have been dead wrong. Having life insurance to give your family gives you the license to spend your retirement money. Remember, you did not put money in your 401(k) for your kids! You were saving it for *your* retirement, so do that! Spend every last dime. Let life insurance go to your kids – for pennies on the dollar, I might add.

I also showed you how to give more to your grandchildren and to charities; how to protect against the loss of a Social Security benefit, and even to cover final expenses; and I hope you remember the story of the widow who thought she was a "millionaire" but found out that her million dollars would provide an income of only about $38,000 per year. I shared some special tips for those who haven't saved enough money, for women, and for non-traditional couples.

Modern retirees have longer life spans today, more ways to secure retirement income, and more post-career employment options than any former generation of retirees. All of these options and opportunities can be incorporated into my seven step retirement plan.

But, in order for the Don't Worry, Retire Happy strategy to work, there is one key decision that you absolutely have to make up front: You must decide right from the beginning that you will enjoy a happy and worry-free retirement.

Odds are that making this decision will help you to feel more confident overall about retiring as you grow into the most rewarding period of your life. There is nothing better than knowing that you are enjoying the lifestyle that you've envisioned for your retirement – happy and worry free!

I can't tell you if the stock market will go up or down, and I can't tell you if we will see inflation or deflation in the future. I don't know! But what I can tell you is this: If you follow my steps, you will:

- Have a retirement plan
- Maximize your Social Security benefits
- Work a little longer and save a little more

- Optimize the rest of your savings to protect from inflation
- Cover your basic expenses with guaranteed lifetime income
- Incorporate a plan for potential long-term care expenses
- Use your home equity wisely

By doing these things, you will have a successful retirement, of that I am sure.

I hope that you have found my seven step plan helpful. There is a lot of information out there today about retirement, but most of it focuses only on saving, which is just one part of the equation, with very little on how to turn those savings into income.

In order to have a successful retirement, you must incorporate all of these steps. With the proper amount of income, along with ample growth and protection, you will be truly able to sit back, not worry, and Retire Happy!

Sources

INTRODUCTION

Hegna, Tom, *Paychecks and Playchecks*, Boston: Acanthus Publishing, 2011.

Bernstein, William, "A Simple Math Formula for Retirement Happiness,"*The Experts RSS*.

The Northwestern Mutual Life Insurance Company, "2012 Planning and Progress Study: 'Financial Discipline & Happiness in Retirement,' Milwaukee, WI: Northwestern Mutual, 2014. Available at: **http://www. northwesternmutual.com/news-room/Documents/2014%20Planning%20 and%20Progress_Financial%20Discipline%20and%20Happiness%20 in%20Retirement.pdf**

Clements, Jonathan, "The Secret to a Happier Retirement: Friends, Neighbors and a Fixed Annuity," *The Wall Street Journal*, 27 July 2005.

Butricia, Barbara S., "The Disappearing Defined Benefit Pension and Its Potential Impact on the Retirement Incomes of Baby Boomers," *The Disappearing Defined Benefit Pension and Its Potential Impact on the Retirement Incomes of Baby Boomers*. SSA Administration.

Feature, Tom ValeoWebMD, "Growing Old, Baby-Boomer Style," *WebMD*. WebMD.

Arnold, Roger, "Why Japan Is Doomed to Insolvency," Real Money.

Dubner, Stephen, "How to Live Longer: A New Marketplace Podcast," *Freakonomics RSS*, 10 Jan. 2013.

Kadlec, Dan, "Lifetime Income Stream Key to Retirement Happiness," *Business Money,* Time Magazine, 30 July 2012.

Nyce, Steve, and Quade, Billie Jean, "Annuities and Retirement Happiness," *Towers Watson*.

STEP 1: WHAT IS YOUR PLAN?

"The Hartford Investments and Retirement Survey: December 2009," *The Hartford*, 2009, **http://www.hartfordinvestor.com/general_pdf/ Hartford_Retirement_Survey_09.pdf.**

"Social Security," *The United States Administration.*

US Department of Health and Human Services, "Who Needs Care?" LongTermCare.gov, longtermcare.gov/the-basics/who-needs-care/

David Blanchett, "Estimating the True Cost of Retirement," Morningstar Investment Management, November 5, 2013.

Duncan Hood, "Retirement: A Number You'll Love," *MoneySense,* April 14, 2008, **www.moneysense.ca/retire/retirement-a-number-youll-love**

"Searching Questions," Oxford Financial Group, Inc., June 2013, **http://www.oxfordfinancialgroup.com/oxfordfinancialgroup. aspx?MyMenu=home&MyPage=freeform10.asp&SessionID=205544422.**

John H. Curry, *Preparing a Secure Retirement: Expert Insight and Advice on Implementing the Secure Retirement Method* (Published & Distributed by: John H. Curry, Tallahassee, FL 2009), p. 11-12.

Tom Hegna, *Retirement Income Masters: Secrets of the Pros* (Acanthus Publishing: Boston, 2013) p.167.

STEP 2: MAXIMIZE SOCIAL SECURITY BENEFITS

The Wall Street Journal. Journal Report. June 22, 2014.
Elaine Floyd, "The Baby Boomer's Guide to Social Security," Horsesmouth, LLC, 2013. (Prudential Presentation).

Mary Beth Franklin, *Maximizing Your Clients' Social Security Retirement Benefits. Answers to the Top 25 Questions about Complicated Claiming Strategies That Every Adviser Needs to Know,* eBook, p. 8-9.

"Reviewing Your Social Security Benefit Options: How a 'Restricted Application' Strategy Can Help You Reach Your Retirement Income Goals," Prudential, 2013.

Floyd, "The Baby Boomer's Guide to Social Security."

"Social Security Survivors Benefits," Social Security Administration, **http://www.ssa.gov/pubs/EN-05-10084.pdf**

"Retirement Security: Challenges for Those Claiming Social Security Benefits Early and New Health Coverage Options," US Government

Accountability Office, April 2014,
http://www.gao.gov/assets/670/662727.pdf.

The Board of Trustees, Federal Old-Age and Survivors Insurance and
Disability Insurance Trust Funds, "The 2010 Annual Report of the Board
of Trustees of the Federal Old-Age and Survivors Insurance and Federal
Disability Insurance Trust Funds," US Government Printing Office, August
9, 2010, http://www.socialsecurity.gov/oact/TR/2010/tr2010.pdf.

STEP 3: EXPLORE A HYBRID RETIREMENT

Romina Boccia, "Working into Retirement: What Washington Can Do,"
The Hill, June 12, 2014, http://thehill.com/blogs/pundits-blog/209018-
working-into-retirement-what-washington-can-do.

Andrew G. Biggs, "What Workers Need to Know About Social Security as
They Plan for Retirement," American Enterprise Institute, July 29, 2014.

Ruth Helman, Nevin Adams, Craig Copeland, Jack VanDerhei, "The 2014
Retirement Confidence Survey: Confidence Rebounds – for Those with
Retirement Plans," *ERBI Issue Briefs* 397 (2014).

Elizabeth Olsen, "Retirees Turn Entrepreneur, Often Scaling Up a Hobby,"
The New York Times, May 14, 2013,
http://www.nytimes.com/2013/05/15/business/retirementspecial/retirees-
turn-entrepreneur-often-scaling-up-a-hobby.html?_r=0.

"Retirement Planner: Getting Benefits While Working," Social Security
Administration, http://www.ssa.gov/retire2/whileworking.htm.

STEP 4: PROTECT YOUR SAVINGS FROM INFLATION

The Retirement Income Reference Book, (LIMRA, 2012).
"Annuity Ladder," *Investopedia*, 2014,
www.investopedia.com/terms/a/annuity-ladder.asp.

"Inflation-Linked Savings Bonds (I Bonds)," *Investopedia*, 2014,
http://www.investopedia.com/terms/i/inflation-linkedsavingsbonds.asp.

STEP 5: SECURE MORE GUARANTEED LIFETIME INCOME

Richard P. Austin, "Living Too Long with Too Little Money:

A 'New Era' for Retirement Planning Payout Annuities - Myths and Realities," *Retirement Planning* (2002).
Dan Kadlec, "Lifetime Income Stream Key to Retirement Happiness," *TIME*, July 30, 2012. **http://business.time.com/2012/07/30/lifetime-income-stream-key-to-retirement-happiness.**

"MetLife Retirement Income IQ Study: A Survey of Pre-Retiree Knowledge of Financial Retirement Issues," MetLife, 2008. **https://www.metlife.com/assets/cao/mmi/publications/studies/mmi-retirement-income-iq.pdf.**

Kelly Greene, "Say Goodbye to the 4% Rule," *The Wall Street Journal*, March 3, 2013. **http://online.wsj.com/news/articles/SB10001424127887324162304578304491492559684.**

Darla Mercado, "The magic withdrawal number in a low-interest-rate retirement? You'll be surprised," *InvestmentNews*, February 7, 2013. **http://www.investmentnews.com/article/20130207/FREE/130209947/the-magic-withdrawal-number-in-a-low-interest-rate-retirement-youll.**

Jonathan Clements, "How to Survive Retirement -- Even if You're Short on Savings," *The Wall Street Journal*, January 17, 2007. **http://online.wsj.com/news/articles/SB116899974081778389.**

Walter Updegrave, "Using Immediate Annuities to Guarantee Retirement Income," *The Wall Street Journal*, July 4, 2014. **http://online.wsj.com/articles/using-immediate-annuities-to-guarantee-retirement-income-1404482404.**

"Income Annuities Improve Portfolio Outcomes in Retirement," Financial Research Corporation, December 2012.
"Retirement Security: Trends in Marriage, Work, and Pensions May Increase Vulnerability for Some Retirees," United States Government Accountability Office, March 5, 2014.

"Annuities and Retirement Happiness," Towers Watson, September 2012. **http://www.towerswatson.com/en-US/Insights/Newsletters/Americas/insider/2012/Annuities-and-Retirement-Happiness.**

Christie Mueller, "Mueller & Associates," **www.christiemueller.com.**
Updegrave, "The Hunt for Guaranteed Lifetime Income," *The Wall Street Journal* July 4, 2014. **http://online.wsj.com/news/articles/SB20001424052702304344504580001471392015864.**

Updegrave, "Using Immediate Annuities to Guarantee Retirement Income." "Bob Hartman, CLU, ChFC, CASL," New York Life, www.bobhartman.com.

McKnight, David. *The Power of Zero: How to Get to the 0% Tax Bracket and Transform Your Retirement*, Boston: Acanthus, 2014.

Moshe A. Milevsky, "Real Longevity Insurance with a Deductible: Introduction to Advanced-Life Delayed Annuities," 2004. http://www.ifid.ca/pdf_workingpapers/WP2004FEB_.pdf

Anne Tergesen, "401(k)s face 'crisis,' says Nobelist Merton," *MarketWatch*, June 24, 2014, http://blogs.marketwatch.com/encore/2014/06/24/401ks-face-crisis-says-nobelist-merton/?mod=WSJBlog.

STEP 6: YOU MUST HAVE A PLAN FOR LONG-TERM CARE

"Medicare at a Glance," The Henry J. Kaiser Family Foundation, September 2, 2014. http://kff.org/medicare/fact-sheet/medicare-at-a-glance-fact-sheet.

"Part A costs," Medicare.gov. http://www.medicare.gov/your-medicare-costs/part-a-costs/part-a-costs.html.

Barry Rand, "Challenges of Long-Term Care," *AARP Bulletin*, November 2013. http://www.aarp.org/home-family/caregiving/info-10-2013/long-term-care-caregiving-rand.html.

The Retirement Income Reference Book, (Hartford, CT: LIMRA, 2012), p. 94. "Genworth 2014 Cost of Care Survey: Home Care Providers, Adult Day Health Care Facilities, Assisted Living Facilities and Nursing Homes," Genworth, 2014. https://www.genworth.com/dam/Americas/US/PDFs/Consumer/corporate/130568_032514_CostofCare_FINAL_nonsecure.pdf.

"Your Medicare Coverage," Medicare.gov, http://www.medicare.gov/coverage/skilled-nursing-facility-care.html.

"Medicare at A Glance." *Medicare at a Glance*. The Henry J. Kaiser Family Foundation, 02 Sept. 2014.
Centers for Medicare and Medicaid Services, "Medicare & You," (Baltimore, MD: US Department of Health and Human Services, 2014), p. 33.

"Safe Ways to Spend Down Your Assets to Qualify for Medicaid," NOLO, http://www.nolo.com/legal-encyclopedia/safe-ways-spend-down-your-assets-qualify-medicaid.html.

STEP 7: USE HOME EQUITY WISELY

"Reverse Mortgage Market Currently at $4.3 Trillion, Less than 1% Penetrated, According to the NRMLA/Hollister Reverse Mortgage Market Index," NMRLA, Hollister Group LLC, June 28, 2007. http://www.nrmlaonline.org/App_Assets/public/7169eab9-fc1d-4a8f-939f-ec029f5e9d3c/RMMI%20Release%20Final%2006-28-07%204.pdf

Jason Oliva "CNN Money: Reverse Mortgages Poised to Be Mainstream Strategy," *ReverseMortgageDaily*, May 20, 2014. http://reversemortgagedaily.com/2014/05/20/cnn-money-reverse-mortgages-poised-to-be-mainstream-strategy.

"Your Guide to Reverse Mortgages," The National Reverse Mortgage Lenders Association, http://www.reversemortgage.org/GettingStarted.aspx. "HUD.gov," US Department of Housing and Urban Development, http://portal.hud.gov/hudportal/HUD.

"Consumer Fact Sheet for Home Equity Conversion Mortgages (HECM)," Federal Housing Administration, US Department of Housing and Urban Development, 2010, http://portal.hud.gov/hudportal/documents/huddoc?id=DOC_13006.pdf.

SOME EXTRA TIPS FOR THOSE WHO HAVE STARTED LATE

"Early or Late Retirement?" Social Security Administration, http://www.ssa.gov/oact/quickcalc/early_late.html#late.

Mary Beth Franklin, "No 4: Little Savings for Retirement," *Kiplinger*, September 2008, http://www.kiplinger.com/article/retirement/T047-C000-S002-no-4-little-savings-for-retirement.html.

A SPECIAL NOTE TO WOMEN

David F. Babbel, "Lifetime Income for Women: A Financial Economist's Perspective," Wharton Financial Institutions Center Policy Brief: Personal Finance, July 31, 2008, http://fic.wharton.upenn.edu/fic/Policy%20page/RetirementIncome-Women.pdf.

Employee Benefits Research Institute
"Women and Retirement Savings," United States Department of Labor,
www.dol.gov/ebsa/publications/women.html.

"The New American Family: The MetLife Study of Family Structure and
Financial Well-Being," MetLife Mature Market Institute, September 2012.
https://www.metlife.com/assets/cao/mmi/publications/studies/2012/
studies/mmi-american-family-structure-finacial-considerations.pdf.

"Retirement Security: Women Still Face Challenges. Report to the
Chairman, Special Committee on Aging, U.S. Senate," Government
Accountability Office, July 2012.

"Understanding the Impact of Family Caregiving on Work," AARP Public
Policy Institute, 2012. http://www.aarp.org/content/dam/aarp/research/
public_policy_institute/ltc/2012/understanding-impact-family-caregiving-
work-AARP-ppi-ltc.pdf.

Barbara A. Butrica and Karen E. Smith, "The Retirement Prospects
of Divorced Women," U.S. Social Security Administration, Office of
Retirement and Disability Policy, 2012.
http://www.ssa.gov/policy/docs/ssb/v72n1/v72n1p11.html.

"Retirement Planner: Benefits for Your Divorced Spouse," Social Security
Administration, http://www.ssa.gov/retire2/yourdivspouse.htm.
Meghan Casserly, "Retirement Planning and Its Challenges for
Women," Forbes, February 9, 2011. http://www.forbes.com/sites/
meghancasserly/2011/02/09/retirement-planning-and-its-challenges-
for-women.

Eric Stallard, "Estimates of the Incidence, Prevalence, Duration, Intensity
and Cost of Chronic Disability among the U.S. Elderly,"North American
Actuarial Journal 15 (2011): 32.

The Retirement Income Reference Book (LIMRA: Hartford, CT 2012), p. 79.
Mary Quist-Newins and Jill B. McCullough, "Strengthening the Retirement
Planning Bridge: Helping the Financial Services Industry Meet the Needs of
Women Business Owners," LIMRA's MarketFacts Quarterly 2 (2012).

Danielle Andrus, "Small Business Owners Underprepared for Retirement
- Female business owners are especially vulnerable," ThinkAdvisor,
February 29, 2012.

http://www.thinkadvisor.com/2012/02/29/small-business-owners-underprepared-for-retirement.
Quist-Newins and McCullough, "Strengthening the Retirement Planning Bridge."

RETIREMENT ISSUES FOR NON-TRADITIONAL COUPLES

"Wealth Transfers for Domestic Partners," College for Financial Planning, 2010. (Course Topic for Accredited Domestic Partnership Advisor Program).

One hundred fourth Congress, "H.R.3396 – Defense Of Marriage Act," http://thomas.loc.gov/cgi-bin/query/z?c104:H.R.3396.ENR:. "After DOMA: What It Means for You," Freedom to Marry, http://www.freedomtomarry.org/resources/entry/after-doma-what-it-means-for-you"

19 States with Legal Gay Marriage and 31 States with Same-Sex Marriage Bans," Gay Marriage Pros and Cons, http://gaymarriage.procon.org/view.resource.php?resourceID=004857.

"Important Information for Same-Sex Couples," Social Security Administration, www.socialsecurity.gov/people/same-sexcouples/.

"Accredited Domestic Partnership Advisor or ADPA," College of Financial Planning, http://www.cffpdesignations.com/Designation/ADPA.

USING "LONGEVITY CREDITS" FOR RETIREMENT INCOME

Parsonex, http://parsonexfranchise.com/parsonex-financial-services-franchise-our-industry.

"Income Annuities Improve Portfolio Outcomes in Retirement," Financial Research Corporation, December 2012.

WHAT DOES LIFE INSURANCE HAVE TO DO WITH RETIREMENT?

"Income Annuities Improve Portfolio Outcomes in Retirement," Financial Research Corporation, December 2012.

Terry Sheriden, "10 Facts Funeral Directors May Not Tell You,"

Bankrate.com, April 11, 2013. http://www.foxbusiness.com/personal-finance/2013/04/11/10-facts-funeral-directors-may-not-tell/.

William Scott Page, "The Life Insurance Industry's Big Secret," *Huffington Post,* December 4, 2012. http://www.huffingtonpost.com/wm-scott-page/the-life-insurance-indust_b_1937246.html.

Daniel Bortz, "When Should You Purchase Life Insurance?" *U.S. News*, July 23, 2012. http://money.usnews.com/money/personal-finance/articles/2012/07/23/when-should-you-purchase-life-insurance.

"Term Life Insurance Policies," Money-Zine.com,. http://www.money-zine.com/financial-planning/buying-insurance/term-life-insurance-policies/.